THE GIFT OF THE OTHER

Mary Deems Howland

The Gift of the Other

Gabriel Marcel's Concept
of Intersubjectivity in Walker Percy's Novels

Duquesne University Press
Pittsburgh, Pennsylvania

Copyright © 1990 by Duquesne University Press

Published by:

Duquesne University Press
600 Forbes Avenue
Pittsburgh, Pennsylvania 15282

Library of Congress Cataloging-in-Publication Data
Howland, Mary Deems, 1940–
    The gift of the other: Gabriel Marcel's concept of
intersubjectivity in Walker Percy's novels / Mary Deems Howland.
        p.   cm.
    Includes bibliographical references.
    ISBN 0–8207–0211–0
    1. Percy, Walker, 1916–   –Philosophy. 2. Marcel, Gabriel,
1889–1973–Influence–Percy. 3. Intersubjectivity in literature.
4. Philosophy in literature. I. Title.
PS3566.E6912Z735   1989
813'.54–dc20   89–38591
                                                                         CIP

Printed in the United States
of America

Contents

Acknowledgments

This study has occupied my inner life for many years. It began as a dissertation under the direction of one of Percy's most perceptive and untiring readers, Lewis A. Lawson. Much of what it has become is due to his guidance. When I first encountered Percy in a graduate seminar at the University of Maryland, only *The Moviegoer*, *The Last Gentleman* and *Love in the Ruins* had been published. *Lancelot* appeared the following year, and then, when I was in the midst of writing about intersubjectivity, *The Second Coming*. Finally, as I was nearing a complete revision of this book, *The Thanatos Syndrome* was published. The novelist continues to frustrate the critic, and the mixed emotions—delight at another novel to join the growing corpus, frustration at never being quite caught up—are perhaps always the lot of anyone who works with a living writer.

I am grateful to many people who have supported my work. My greatest professional debt is to Lewis A. Lawson, whose attention to detail and genuine love of ideas has thoroughly influenced my reading of Percy. It was he who first suggested that I might read Gabriel Marcel.

Colleagues at the United States Naval Academy have graciously given me their ears and have encouraged me when my strength was flagging. I am especially grateful to Molly Tinsley for her friendship and encouragement and to David White, whose interest in Walker Percy has stimulated my own. Carol Burke, Director of the Writing Center, has put me back on course more than once. Laurence Mazzeno, the outgoing chair of the English Department, has been of invaluable assistance in finding support for this project. I am grateful for a grant from the United States Naval Academy

Research Council which allowed me to work on the final chapter of this book.

My students over the last five years have kept me aware of how provocative Percy's ideas are. Their willingness to argue with me has made this book stronger because I have been forced to reexamine my own ideas in the light of their comments. They have responded with great enthusiasm to Percy's novels, suggesting that Percy's voice speaks across generations and is truly contemporary, perfectly capturing the nuances of our times.

My editors at Duquesne University Press have proven once again how valuable response is to the writer. They have shown me both where what I thought was clear was murky and where my argument made sense. I am especially grateful to Susan B. Wadsworth, who expertly saw the work through to completion.

I have been most fortunate in having the loving support and interest of my family: my parents to whom this book is dedicated and my (now grown) children, Stephen and Susan, who remember the origins of this project, and who frequently inquire after its health. My deepest thanks go to my husband, Vaughn Howland, who has put up with a good deal while I have insisted on chaining myself to the word processor. Vaughn has surprised me many times in our years together, but never so much as when he demonstrated his editorial skills and his willingness to read chapters. He has taught me how very important the *other* is.

Finally, I owe a special debt to Walker Percy for the gift of novels which have spoken to me when I was most in need of counsel. Even the rigors of critical analysis cannot dampen the pleasure I continue to take in his novelistic explorations of what it is to live a life. Percy's unfailing humor, humanity and spiritual depth reach out to the reader and engage him or her in the ongoing journey which is each person's life.

Walker Percy & Gabriel Marcel

Intersubjectivity and World

Friends of Walker Percy in the thirties would have had little reason to suspect that he would become a novelist, let alone that he would become a major literary voice—a voice concerned both personally and philosophically with modern anxiety over the old systems of life which seem to have broken down and new ones that have yet to be defined. As an undergraduate at the University of North Carolina, he majored in chemistry in preparation for medical school, and in 1941, he received his M.D. from Columbia University. But in 1942, Percy contracted tuberculosis while working as a pathologist at Bellevue Hospital, and the course of his life was changed. Percy would later admit, in an interview with John Griffin Jones, that tuberculosis provided him with the "respectable excuse" to change his life, calling the disease "the best thing that ever happened to me because it gave me a chance to quit medicine."[1] Following this happy fall, Percy went to Saranac Lake in New York, where he took the cure and turned to literature and philosophy: "For two years I could read anything. I read for two years."[2]

Among the most profound influences on Percy's contemplative life at Saranac Lake were Dostoevski's novels, especially *Notes from Underground*, which led him to existentialist philosophers, including Sören Kierkegaard, whose books were just appearing in English translation. Percy has described the intellectual breakthrough he experienced during this period of convalescence:

> I saw one day . . . that science can say so much about things, objects or people, but by its very method, by its own self-imposed limitation, the scientific method can only utter a statement about a single

object, a glass or a frog or a dogfish—or a man—only insofar as it resembles other things of its kind . . . Science can say everything about a man except what he is in himself.[3]

Percy has never repudiated the scientific method; indeed he maintains an appreciation for its beauty and clarity. Nevertheless, he has argued that questions about values in human life, or those involved with how to live in a century "where science is triumphant," are beyond the reach of the scientific method.[4] Thus, knowing that science did not hold the answers to the questions that most concerned him, questions about our place in a world where we seem to be disfranchised, Percy began to shift from a search for scientific facts to a philosophical and religious search for meaning.

As Percy has readily confessed, the direction of his search was greatly influenced by the works of such existentialists as Kierkegaard, Martin Heidegger, Jean-Paul Sartre, and Gabriel Marcel.[5] The growing body of criticism on Percy's novels has confirmed his special indebtedness to Kierkegaard, but there has been little exploration of the equally important debt to Marcel. Yet Percy himself often acknowledges that he was significantly influenced by Marcel. In virtually every interview in which he discusses the writers and philosophers who have contributed to his developing thought, he mentions Gabriel Marcel. For example, to Harriet Doar he declares: "The following writers have meant most to me and in this order: Dostoevski, Kierkegaard, St. Augustine, Lawrence, Joyce, Gerard Hopkins, Marcel."[6] As for the relation between the novel and ideas, Percy frequently acknowledges his debt to the French existentialists: "I use the fiction form as a vehicle for incarnating ideas, as did Jean Paul Sartre and Gabriel Marcel."[7] Moreover, in response to a question on the writers with whom he felt most compatible, Percy says, "I was always closer to Frenchmen like Sartre or Camus or Marcel."[8] Thus, from one context to another, Percy repeatedly invokes the name of Marcel as an indispensable source of his thought as it finds expression in his novels.

In temperament and conviction, Percy is closer to Gabriel Marcel than to any of the other existentialists. Although he has studied Kierkegaard and has employed a number of Kierkegaardian ideas in his novels, Percy describes in an interview with Bradley R. Dewey a deficiency that he finds in the Danish philosopher's thinking:

> Kierkegaard seemed to set up subjectivity as the only alternative [to Hegel's objectivity]. That has always bothered me, because I think he is falling into the trap of emotion, inwardness, and so forth, yet never makes any provisions, as far as I can tell, for understanding or an explanation of intersubjectivity—caring for the other person, or how to know other people.[9]

In Gabriel Marcel, Percy found a philosopher who mediates between Kierkegaardian subjectivity and Hegelian objectivity through the concept of *intersubjectivity*, which allows persons perceived as an "I" and "thou" to share and affirm the world.

Walker Percy's reading of Marcel has been neither cursory nor of short term interest. There are as many references to Marcel's thought in Percy's later essays as in his earlier ones, a span also reflected in the novels. In his novels, the question of whether intersubjectivity develops or fails to develop becomes the pivotal issue for characters who struggle to find a meaningful way to live. Therefore, as indicated in his earliest published essay, "Symbol As Need" (1954), Percy affirms Marcel's metaphysical opposition to Descartes[10] which is best distilled in a passage in *The Mystery of Being*: "It is not enough to say that it is a metaphysic of being; it is a metaphysic of *we are* as opposed to a metaphysic of *I think*."[11] Although the Cartesian *cogito* (the epistemological self) is capable of making enormous scientific and mathematical progress, it is ultimately lonely for the created world and haunts its own body like a ghost in a machine.[12] Restoring a sense of community and participation with others, Marcel shows how human beings can reach out to others and regain their ontological position in the physical world.

Percy has also shown great interest in Marcel's view that language is an intersubjective medium. In *The Mystery of Being*, Marcel asserts that intersubjectivity is "the mysterious root of language" (*MB* 2: 12). He goes on to mention one of his recurring concerns: words wear out under constant usage, and they may conceal the very meaning they intend to reveal. As Marcel explains:

> I have had the misfortune to note by my own experience that when we adhere to this expression of intersubjective nexus, what I am tempted to call a mental clot is formed, which interrupts the circulation of thought. . . . I mean that the words, so to say, interpose

themselves between me and the thought I am driving at; they get a bogey-like and unwelcome reality of their own; they become an obstacle instead of remaining an instrument (*MB* 2: 12–13).

In his essay "A Novel About the End of the World," Percy echoes Marcel in his description of the modern human, who is "a caricature of the contemporary Cartesian man," so abstracted from the self that "all creaturely relations crumble at his touch." As soon as Percy's modern man speaks, his abstract language becomes meaningless because it fails to name: "He has but to utter a word—*achieving intersubjectivity, interpersonal relations, meaningful behavior*—and that which the word signifies vanishes."[13] Marcel did not want his ideas, his formulations of what he saw as truth, to come between him and reality, because he understood the danger in theoretical constructs—that once one creates a structure through which to view the world of experience, the abstract concept tends to take on a life of its own, to form a hard shell around itself so that it no longer names something in the world because it loses its underpinnings in lived experience.

Just as individuals are always in danger of retreating within the self, where they are held prisoner by their own self-absorption, so ideas and theoretical constructs may lose their ability to name reality soon after they are framed. Aware of the reductionist tendency in all theoretical constructs, Marcel believed that philosophy must remain an investigative endeavor, the philosopher scrupulously avoiding abstract formulations that lead to losing contact with everyday life.

In both his philosophical essays and his plays, Marcel focuses on the day-to-day encounters that the individual has with other individuals. Pointing to our tendency to cut ourselves off from others and our concomitant need for other people, Marcel stresses the value of the ordinary interchanges that people experience in the family, the business world and the church. No individual is ever completely cut off from others, even though to live an authentic existence is a struggle, requiring real effort on the part of the individual to remain open, to search out those "others" who can be loved. As Marcel sees it, one never ceases to be *homo viator*, one who must search for ways to become more open to the ambiguous but real ontological presence that surrounds the individual like a sea. The victory for Marcel lies in the search itself, a search made in hope and good faith, and most importantly, a search made in the company of other people.

The origin of Marcel's philosophy of our intersubjective need for one another most obviously derives from his dissertation study of Josiah Royce. In Royce's idea of the "beloved community," Marcel could invest his idealism. But it was from his experiences in World War I that Marcel was able to discover actual flesh for Royce's idea, as well as to begin straying from his predecessor's idealism. Excused from active duty because of his health, Marcel became the head of the Red Cross Information Service in August 1914. He was responsible for getting news of the wounded and answering inquiries from people who had lost touch with sons, brothers and husbands. In this painful and concrete position, Marcel had his belief in the importance of the individual life constantly reinforced:

> Every day I received personal visits from the unfortunate relatives who implored us to obtain what information we could so that in the end every index card was to me a heart-rending personal appeal. Nothing, I think, could have immunized me better against the power of effacement possessed by the abstract terms which fill the reports of journalists and historians of the war.[14]

Rather than idealistically abstracting himself, Marcel recognized that his approach to the families of missing soldiers had to be wholly personal:

> Whenever I could, I made a point of seeing personally those who came to make inquiries and, far from treating them as mere cases from the files, did my best to show them the greatest possible sympathy. This gave me the opportunity of coming into contact with many people from all walks of life and of making a constant effort to put myself in their place, in order to imagine the anguish which they all shared but which underwent subtle transformations in each of them. It is against this background of deep distress that each questionnaire, each inquiry stood out.[15]

From this passage, we also see that Marcel discovered the inadequacy of questionnaires filled out by the families to capture the complex identities of the missing soldiers. In *The Moviegoer*,

Walker Percy too will stress the failure of questionnaires and the various licenses, credit cards and identity cards we carry to tell us anything whatsoever about who we are. Binx Bolling claims to take great pleasure in responding to questionnaires—"I enjoy answering polls as much as anyone and take pleasure in giving intelligent replies to all questions." Although Binx remarks of the credit cards and other forms of identification he collects, "It is a pleasure to carry out the duties of a citizen and to receive in return a receipt or a neat styrene card with one's name on it certifying, so to speak, one's right to exist," Binx's words are ironic because he has no sense of who he is or what to do with his life.[16] William Rodney Allen points out that Binx will have to look beyond such "existentially inauthentic indicators of identity" as his identification and credit cards to define himself as a self.[17]

Marcel's first two books, *Metaphysical Journal* and *Being and Having*, are enlightening in relation to Percy, because the journal form affords Marcel the freedom to develop his nonsystematic philosophy. Although the entries appear in chronological order, the thought frequently moves backward as Marcel rereads earlier entries, fills out points, redefines terms, contemplates old solutions anew, reviews and alters a previously introduced concept. The writing becomes a record and an intimation at the same time, a journey undertaken and still in progress. Like the travel journals of earlier explorers, Marcel's philosophical journals are full of the excitement of being *en route*, of new ground to reconnoiter, and of the enormous risk and possible fulfillment of such journeying. As we shall see, the techniques of Marcel's journalizing will have a significant influence on Percy's novels.

So much did Marcel see his philosophy as process and not product, a journey undertaken rather than a city built, that the journey metaphor is by far the most prominent in his writings. In a lecture included in *Being and Having*, for example, Marcel discusses his conversion to Catholicism "after a winding and intricate journey."[18] Far from regretting the difficult journey, Marcel notes that his own struggle provided him with empathy for other wayfarers, "groping souls, travellers and seekers" (*BH* 199). He goes on to express his most deeply felt credo: "For I believe that no man, however enlightened and holy he is, can ever really arrive until the others, *all* the others, have started out to follow him" (*BH* 199–200). Inseparable from other people, Marcel's philosophy serves as an invocation for companionship on his quest. He therefore conceives his audience not as people to be instructed but as fellow travellers with an interest equally as vital as his own in finding out what it is to be an incarnated being in the situations of life.[19]

A brief look at Marcel's thinking about incarnation provides the necessary ground for tracing his description of the human condition and the intersubjective nature of his philosophical journey. Marcel argues that one's incarnation in a body is an absolute requirement for being in the world. "My body" is interposed between "me" and the world: "I only *am* my body more absolutely than I am anything else because to be anything else whatsoever I need first of all to make use of my body."[20] Although I may view my body as an object, it is more to me than an object among other objects in the world because it is *my* body and not someone else's:

> It is in relation to me as conscious of my body, that is to say as grasping it at one and the same time as object (body) and as non-object (my body) that all existence is defined. In a word, to state the existence of a being or of a thing would be to say: This being is of the same nature as my body and belongs to the same world (*MJ* 315).

Only by understanding the complicated relationship that he has with his body can Marcel make sense of his ontological position in the world. The question "What is my relationship with my body?" cannot be truthfully answered by saying "I *am* a body." Nor can it be answered by saying "I *have* a body." Neither statement alone is true. Accordingly, Marcel argues that the primary assumption involved with incarnation, not Descartes's *cogito*, is the basic given of existence:

> Incarnation—the central 'given' of metaphysic. Incarnation is the situation of a being who appears to himself to be, as it were *bound* to a body. This 'given' is opaque to itself: opposition to the *cogito*. Of this body, I can neither say that it is I, nor that it is not I, nor that it is *for* me (object). The opposition of subject and object is found to be transcended from the start (*BH* 11–12).

From the privileged relationship that the individual has with the body are derived all potential relations with the rest of creation, both the world of objects and the world of other people.

By having a body, the individual participates in the world of objects. Only by virtue of having a body is it possible for one to have anything else: "the mysterious relation uniting me to my body is at the foundation of all my powers of having" (*BH* 84). One's body is, however, not an ordinary possession that one can dispose of, which raises what for Camus is the initial question in life or philosophy: suicide. Marcel sensibly argues that we are so intimately linked to our bodies that we cannot dispose of the body without losing the ability to dispose of it: "I have only the absolute disposal of my life. . . . if I put myself in such a condition that I can never dispose of it again; here we meet the irrevocable" (*BH* 87). Having a body connects the individual subject to a larger realm of being, because it is only as a result of incarnation that anyone can participate in the world with other people who are themselves incarnated beings. My relationship with my body, then, helps me to understand my being in the world with others who bear the same mysterious relationship to their bodies.

Walker Percy takes Marcel's phenomenological study of the relationship between "I" and "my body" and uses it in his novels as a constant reminder of the individual's ontological status in the world. Engaged as they are in self-absorbed ratiocinations and philosophical musings, Percy's main characters are often in danger of losing their awareness of being embodied. They risk becoming "all mind" to the detriment of their ontological presence in the world. Thus Percy's protagonists are frequently recalled to awareness of the body, as when, for example, Binx Bolling "comes to himself" after being wounded in Korea: "Six inches from my nose a dung beetle was scratching around in the leaves. As I watched, there awoke in me an immense curiosity. I was onto something."[21] In *The Second Coming*, the pain of an abscessed tooth drives Will Barrett from the cave where he awaits a message from God and back into the world of his fellow creatures. Tom More, the main character of *Love in the Ruins*, realizes that he wants to live only after he comes to on Christmas Eve and see his wrists slashed: "Seeing the blood, I came to myself, saw myself as itself and the world for what it is, and began to love life. . . . After all, why not live?"[22] Only the demented Lancelot maintains a separation from his body, desiring only to see the ocular proof of Margot's infidelity on the videotapes his servant Elgin has made for his viewing. Denying his incarnation, Lancelot is determined to stand apart from physical pain, to reduce it to a problem. Shortly before he blows up his ancestral home, Lance takes two capsules and finds instant relief: "before, I was part of the pain, there was no getting away from it. Now I had some distance. The pain was still there, but I stood off a ways. It became a problem to be solved."[23]

Related to Marcel's ideas on incarnation are the distinctions he draws between "problem" and "mystery," which ultimately bear on the conditions of being and having. For Marcel, to live is to be enmeshed in the mystery of being. In his essay, "On the Ontological Mystery," Marcel contends that we cannot approach a discussion of mystery in the same way we approach a problem.[24] A problem allows the questioner to stand outside the data he examines like a scientist working in the laboratory. Scientists do not consider their relationship to the matter being examined because the scientific method demands that the subject be clearly separated from the object examined. Marcel determines that a problem is "before me in its entirety," whereas a mystery is "something in which I find myself caught up, and whose essence is therefore not to be before me in its entirety" (*BH* 100). When ontological questions are raised, philosophers must realize that they themselves are involved in the Being they question. The Cartesian split between the thinking subject (*res cogitans*) and the object (*res extensa*) cannot represent the proper approach to being because being is a mystery, which Marcel defines as "a problem which encroaches upon its own data, invading them, as it were, and thereby transcending itself as a simple problem" (*PE* 8).[25]

From the vantage of Marcel's logic, a mystery is not something that cannot be solved, but rather the whole configuration of people and situations in which a person is involved, and from which the person can never separate self. It is impossible to retreat to some privileged position beyond that configuration. If, in thought, we force such a separation between ourselves and our lives, we alter the situation by extracting one of the prime elements from it. Finally, we can never get outside our own lives, for if we imagine that we are outside, it is no longer *our* lives that are in question. Marcel therefore argues that we, as individuals, always seem to see ourselves as a problem for which there are no available answers: "I am *always and at every moment* more than the totality of predicates that an enquiry made by myself—or by someone else—about myself would be able to bring to light" (*MJ* 199).

Only by opening ourselves to other people whom we conceive as "thous" can we participate in what Marcel insists is the *mystery* of being. As incarnated creatures, we participate in both having and being, but the realm of being must take precedence, because only by participating in being with others can we fulfill our potential as humans, our destiny as incarnated beings who live in a world with other incarnated beings who are presences for us and for whom we are a presence. Thus, rather than opposites, Marcel's categories of being and having are two ways of integrating the self with all the other objects and selves that constitute the world. Empiricism and scientific objectivity operate in the realm of having inasmuch as the self can temporarily separate itself from the objects under consideration, study them, and provide solutions to the problems they present. For Marcel, knowledge gained from scientific enquiry is a form of having because it is something that a person can give to others: "Knowledge as a mode of having is essentially communicable" (*BH* 145). But when our own lives and relationships with others are under consideration, we are involved in mysteries that necessarily include us, a condition that Marcel calls the "metaproblematic." This is the realm of the mystery in which the self is involved as a nonsubtractable component. Whereas one's relations with objects can be solved because they present problems for which there are discoverable answers, relations with other people and with one's own inner being must be approached by self-involvement with them, through the participation and the spiritual availability of what Marcel calls *disponibilité*.[26] To participate in being, one must recognize and treat other people as *thous*, for in some ultimately ontological and logical sense, it is necessary to grant a reality to others that is more real than one's own being: "Not only do we have a right to assert that others exist, but I should be inclined to contend that existence can be attributed only to others . . . and that I cannot think of myself as existing except insofar as I conceive of myself as not being the others: and so as other than them" (*BH* 104).

Walker Percy frequently employs these categories of problem and mystery in his novels. All Percy's protagonists come to understand, albeit at different levels of awareness, that their own lives are mysteries and that intersubjective relations with others are inaccessible when they attempt to approach others as "problems." Even Lancelot Lamar, who struggles to address his wife's infidelity as a problem, finds the empirical approach to his own life ultimately inadequate. Lance has glimmers of the mysterious nature of his own being. He remarks to Percival/John: "How happy scientists are! Why didn't we become scientists, Percival? They confront problems which can be solved. We don't know what we confront."[27] In *The Second Coming*, Allison Huger is delighted to have the problem of how to move the unconscious Will Barrett: "When he landed on the floor of her greenhouse, knocking himself out, he was a problem to be solved, like moving the stove. Problems are for solving. Alone."[28] But when Will regains consciousness, Allie discovers that this assessment is inadequate; Will is a mysterious presence whom she must approach as a "thou."

In *The Mystery of Being*, after years devoted to crystallizing the differences between having and being, problem and mystery, Marcel discusses two representative people who operate in the two realms: the scientist in the realm of having and the philosopher in the realm of being. The scientist studies objects in a world from which he has deliberately removed himself: "His task is to bring order into a world which is as little as possible *his own* particular world, which is as much as possible *the* world in general."[29] A valid scientific experiment can be duplicated under similar circumstances in any place, at any time, by any qualified scientist. In the realm of scientific enquiry, what Marcel calls "primary reflection," the kind of thinking that is done by the *cogito* is perfectly in order. Yet primary reflection cannot be brought to bear upon our individual lives and our relations with ourselves and others. Instead, the philosopher employs what Marcel calls "secondary reflection," a kind of thinking that restores the self to the world being contemplated.

Secondary reflection or "recollection" restores the unity of subject and object and looks at the world in which the philosopher himself, by definition, *is*.

Marcel uses the term "recollection" with full understanding of its two English meanings. While recollection involves the exercise of memory, it also entails the re-collection of everything composing the self prior to a reflection upon such ontological issues as the nature of hope, of fidelity, of having a body. According to Marcel, recollection "means what it says—the act whereby I re-collect myself as a unity; but this hold, this grasp upon myself, is also relaxation and abandon" (*PE* 12). Recollection, the invitation to the self to join the reflection upon mysteries in which it is involved, brings one to the threshold of being. Unlike the scientist who stands over against the world being examined, the philosopher must always bear in mind that a person's own participation in being is deeply *intersubjective* in nature.

Marcel insists that once questions about being begin to be asked, the philosopher is involved in an intersubjective world, since "a thought which directs itself toward being, by that very act recreates around itself the intersubjective presence which a philosophy of monadist inspiration begins by expelling in the most arbitrary and high-handed manner" (*MB* 2: 18). We cannot extricate ourselves from the being that surrounds us because there is no available foothold outside of being:

> There is not, and there cannot be, any global abstraction, any final high terrace to which we can climb by means of abstract thought, there to rest forever; for our condition in this world does remain, in the last analysis, that of a wanderer, an itinerant being, who cannot come to absolute rest except by a fiction, a fiction which it is the duty of philosophic reflection to oppose with all its strength (*MB* 1: 164).

Here we return to Marcel's conception of the philosophical human as *homo viator*, a being constrained to search out a personal identity within the larger ontological world of others with whom there is an ineluctable connection:

> The ontological order can only be recognized personally by the whole of a being, involved in a drama which is his own, though it overflows him infinitely in all directions—a being to whom the

strange power has been imparted of asserting or denying himself. He asserts himself insofar as he asserts Being and opens himself to it: or he denies himself by denying Being and thereby closing himself to It. In this dilemma lies the very essence of his freedom (*BH* 120–21).

In "The Ego and Its Relation to Others," Marcel illustrates his contention that awareness of self comes about as a result of the responses of others, that in fact awareness of the self *as* a self is dependent upon the confirmation of some other person. Suggesting that "the most elementary example, the closest to earth, is also the most instructive," Marcel shows that small children discover who they are only because of the responses of others, which means that the ego cannot be defined except through intersubjective activity.[30] Marcel provides a tableau: a young child presents his mother with a bouquet of wild flowers. He notes the triumph and the gesture which accompany the child's gift:

> The child points himself out for affirmation and gratitude: "It was I, I who am with you here, who picked these lovely flowers, don't go thinking it was Nanny or my sister; it was I and *no one else.* . . . Thus the child draws attention to himself, he offers himself to the other in order to receive a special tribute (*HV* 13).

The child who offers *himself* along with his gift of flowers becomes an example of the ego as a "center of magnetism" (*HV* 14), establishing itself as a presence by drawing all attention to itself. Walker Percy will echo this scene of the child and his flowers in the conclusion of *The Moviegoer* when Binx Bolling, having committed himself to caring for Kate, presents her with a cape jasmine as a token of his abiding concern, his gift of self.

Marcel insists that from early childhood the individual's "consciousness of existing . . . is linked up with the urge to make ourselves *recognized* by some other person [who] . . . is needed to integrate the self" (*HV* 14). Furthermore, Marcel invariably demonstrates that the intersubjective world pre-exists the world that one studies objectively: "The more the *ego* realizes that it is but one among others, among an infinity of others with which it maintains relations . . . the more it tends to recapture the feeling of this density [of Being]" (*MB* 2: 19). For Marcel the intersubjective world into which every child is born precedes the Cartesian division of subject-object, just as incarnation precedes cognition of one's having or being a body. Walker Percy agrees with Marcel's placement of intersubjectivity as ontologically prior to all other conditions: "the most radical backtracking into consciousness cannot carry us beyond what Marcel calls the 'intersubjective milieu,' by which he means the prime and irreducible character of intersubjectivity."[31]

Intersubjectivity names the individual self's relationships with others, just as incarnation names its relation to the world. In order to be fully human, the individual must participate in being with those "others" who are in the world. In order for the "I" to say "I am," it must assert simultaneously, "Thou art," thus entering into an intersubjective relation with a "thou." As soon as "I" becomes aware of the other as a presence—"thou"—there cannot exist an objectified third person, a "him" or "her." Obviously, Marcel's notion of "presence" bears critically upon his conception of intersubjectivity. In *The Mystery of Being*, Marcel essays to define presence by contrasting our relationships with other persons to those we have with objects. Fearing that his discussion may turn presence into a kind of "vaporized object," one that "contrasts rather unfavorably with the tangible, solid resistant objects that we are used to in what we call real life," Marcel draws the distinction that, unlike objects, another person's presence "is something which can only be gathered to oneself or shut out from oneself, be welcomed or rebuffed" (*MB* 1: 255). One can seize or appropriate objects, but cannot truly be *with* them. Only the presences of other people can be "evoked or invoked" as the necessary criteria constituting "being" (*MB* 1: 256).

By establishing presence as the defining quality of both the "I" and the "thou," Marcel avoids an extreme subjectivity which would be in danger of excluding the "other" and becoming solipsistic. His alternative to objectivity, therefore, is not subjectivity, but *intersubjectivity*, the mutual participation of subjects with each other in the world: I/thou becomes "we" as compound subject. Nevertheless, Marcel warns that communion between the "I" and the "thou" is by no means inevitable, for the "I" is always in danger of withdrawing into the circle of self, excluding the other. Such a withdrawal or schism not only diminishes self-shared identity or presence but also impinges on language, the vehicle through which we name and affirm a shared world. As Marcel explains, if another person does not appear to an "I" as a thou-presence,

> I may even have the extremely disagreeable feeling that my own words, as he repeats them to me, as he reflects them back at me, have become unrecognizable. By a very singular phenomenon indeed, this stranger interposes himself between me and my own reality, he makes me in some sense also a stranger to myself; I am not really myself when I am with him (*MB* 1: 252).[32]

If, on the other hand, the "I" and the "thou" are open and available to each other as presences, then "thou" reveals "I" to me more fully than "I" am capable of revealing myself to myself.

Ultimately, the intersubjective love of the I and the thou is grounded in the divine love of God, whom Marcel calls the "absolute Thou."[33] Loving communion between individuals depends for its investiture upon God who is Being in all its plenitude. God as absolute Thou is "the guarantee of the union which holds us together, myself to myself, or the one to the other, or these beings to those other beings" (*HV* 60). According to Marcel, love cannot constitute a closed system, because love transcends itself in every direction and "demands for its complete realization a universal communion outside which it cannot be satisfied. . . . this universal communion itself can only be centered upon an absolute Thou" (*HV* 152).

A glance at only a few details in the life of Walker Percy will help to explain his admiration for Gabriel Marcel as a philosophical and spiritual thinker. Percy survived a childhood marked by the loss of both parents. His father, LeRoy Pratt Percy, committed suicide in 1929 when Walker was 13; his mother died in a car accident two years later. Then in January 1942, Percy lost William Alexander Percy, "Uncle Will," his father's first cousin who had adopted Walker and his two younger brothers. That same year Percy contracted tuberculosis and found himself at Saranac Lake. Despite the anchors provided by his marriage to Mary Townsend in 1946, and his conversion to Catholicism the following year, Percy evidently felt in need of a mentor whose worldview he could embrace. When he first read Marcel in the early fifties, Percy must have responded to the very individual voice that he heard, a voice that was at once both similar and contrary to his Uncle Will's.[34] In Marcel, a man of his father's and his uncle's generation, Percy found a philosophy grounded in hope.

Will Percy's influence on his adopted son Walker cannot be overemphasized. Although Walker Percy asserts his differences from his "uncle's" thinking, he stresses how important Will's teachings were to him as "a raw youth from age 14 to 26 . . . whose only talent was a knack for looking and listening." To know Will Percy was "to encounter a complete, articulated view of the world as tragic as it was noble."[35] Walker remembers his uncle's eyes as always "shadowed by sadness," a result no doubt of Will Percy's lifelong attempt to establish a place for himself in the Percy family, to find a way to live his life that would not put his ancestors to shame. Will Percy writes in *Lanterns on the Levee* (1941) that his entry on the historical stage "seemed fairly belated" (126). Born late into an aristocracy which he described as "in the act of dying," Will Percy understood that his class was but a "remnant of the old dispensation" (*LL* 63). The weight of his family's illustrious past bore heavily on Will Percy. His namesake grandfather, Colonel William Alexander Percy, "the gray eagle of the delta," fought with honor in the Civil War; his father, LeRoy Percy, defeated James K. Vardaman and served one term as United States senator from Mississippi.[36] As a young man just out of Harvard Law School, Will Percy felt obliged "to justify the ways of man to God," but he adds immediately, "But how? What does one do with a life, or at any rate intend to do?" (*LL* 126–27). Will Percy's question lies at the very core of his adopted son Walker's novels.

Will Percy was of the generation of Southern sons who lived in the pale afterglow of the age of the heroic grandfathers, a subject that Richard H. King investigates at length.[37] Will Percy never felt that he found an appropriate field of action, despite the fact that he fought in the Argonne in World War I. However, his service at the front provided him with the one time he found life worth living. Although Will hated war and judged himself "desperately unfitted for it by temperament or ability," he admits that the war "had meaning, and daily life hasn't: it was part of a common endeavor, and daily life is isolated and lonely" (*LL* 223). Years later, his adopted son Walker writes: "Why is war man's greatest pleasure?" and then, more personally, "Why is it the only time I ever saw my uncle happy during his entire life was the afternoon of December 7, 1941, when the Japanese bombed Pearl Harbor?"[38]

Thus young Walker, a youth who noticed most of what was going on around him, was impressed by his uncle's melancholy and his tight-lipped stoic endurance. A devotee of Marcus Aurelius, Will Percy believed that the Roman emperor could show him how to live in the face of ultimate destruction: "Under the southern Valhalla the torch has been thrust, already the bastions have fallen. Watching the flames mount, we, scattered remnant of the old dispensation, smile scornfully, but grieve in our hearts" (*LL* 63). In an essay, Walker Percy comments on the limitations of Uncle Will's stoicism: "For the Stoic there is no real hope. His finest hour is to sit tight-lipped and ironic while the world comes crashing down around him."[39] Walker was the son, then, of two despairing fathers: LeRoy Pratt, who ended his life with a 12-gauge Greener shotgun, and William Alexander, who found a reason to live only when he was under fire in the Argonne. Given this legacy, we should not be surprised that the characters in Percy's novels frequently have suicidal tendencies and that they are often attracted to war. But it is most important to notice that Walker Percy offers an alternative when he portrays the human being as Marcel's *homo viator*, whose life is a spiritual journey on an earth that is not the individual's ultimate home. Although never completely safe from the temptation to withdraw, Percy's protagonists find ways to live in the company of beloved others. All is not lost, he assures his readers; war and suicide are not the only solutions to despairing loneliness. Ultimately every sovereign individual must choose between affirmation and despair, as Father Smith explains to Tom More in *The Thanatos Syndrome*: "In the end one must choose— given the chance. . . . Life or death."[40]

Like William Alexander Percy, Gabriel Marcel was a bookish man whose life was forever altered by the first World War. But Marcel found a way out of alienation, a way to escape the loneliness that assailed Will Percy all his life. By coming to see human beings as spiritual wayfarers, and by focusing on the shared consciousness of intersubjectivity, Marcel discovered an avenue for modern humans, a thoroughfare leading from individual isolation toward a reunion and communion with others. In the writings of Marcel and of Will Percy, we can perceive these opposing directions, and a comparison of two passages from their works is instructive. Will Percy ends "Home," the final chapter of *Lanterns on the Levee*, with a meditation in the cemetery in Greenville, Mississippi:

> Here among the graves in the twilight I see one thing only, but I see that thing clear. I see the long wall of a rampart sombre with sunset, a dusty road at its base. On the tower of the rampart stand the glorious high gods, Death and the rest, insolent and watching. Below on the road stream the tribes of men, tired, bent, hurt, and stumbling, and each man alone. As one comes beneath the tower, the High God descends and faces the wayfarer. He speaks three slow words: "Who are you?" The pilgrim I know should be able to straighten his shoulders, to stand his tallest, and to answer defiantly: "I am your son" (*LL* 348).

The tone of this passage is cold and remote. Will Percy's wayfarer is isolated from others; although there are "tribes" of men on the road, there is no camaraderie: each man is alone. Gabriel Marcel also evokes the image of a wayfarer in the conclusion of his final essay in *Homo Viator*:

> In the presence of enemy forces whose devastating action is more widespread each day, on the eve of destruction which can reduce to nothing the people and things we live for, let me invoke this spirit of metamorphosis. . . . Let us allow the hope to penetrate to our hearts that this spirit may transmute us so intimately ourselves that we shall be able to face the desolate prospect with a rejuvenated soul, full of acceptance and in tune with the unfathomable.
>
> Oh spirit of metamorphosis!
>
> When we try to obliterate the frontier of clouds which separates us from the other world, guide our unpracticed movements! And, when the given hour shall strike, arouse us, eager as the traveller who straps on his rucksack while beyond the misty window pane the earliest rays of dawn are faintly visible! (*HV* 270).

Set at dawn, Marcel's passage points toward the future when *homo viator* will journey out with hope, whereas Will Percy's passage is set among the graves at twilight, pointing to the past and imagining a future where the only reward will be for the defiant son to claim kinship with his father. Unlike Will Percy's solitary wayfarer, Marcel's traveller is a member of a community of searchers, evidenced by his use of the plural pronouns, *we* and *us*. Also evident in Will Percy's passage is Marcel's fundamental question, slightly altered. Percy imagines the "high God" asking "Who are you?" and the brave pilgrim's defiant answer, "I am your son." By the same token, Marcel's primary question is the one each individual must ask, "Who am I?" Marcel concludes that this question can be answered solely by the "other" who confirms for each of us our own existence.

A product of the same times that led Will Percy to endure stoically in a world that he believed would ultimately destroy the individual, Gabriel Marcel stressed the permanence of hope. Walker Percy no doubt saw that Marcel's hope does not issue from a facile optimism, but rather from a full awareness of the possibility of despair. Marcel understood the powerful attraction despair can have for the individual, describing despair as "above all things a fascination" and an "enchantment" (*HV* 41, 42). Pressed upon by the death-dealing modern world, the human being is always tempted to despair. Under such circumstances, Marcel suggests that even what ordinarily appears as enthusiasm for life may turn inward against the individual: "the flame turns away from the matter which is its natural food [life], to devour itself. This is what we express admirably when we say of a being 'he preys upon himself.' From this point of view, despair can be compared to a certain spiritual autophagy" (*HV* 44). When a person falls prey to despair, energy that should be turned outward toward participation in being is directed inward, becoming a self-consuming flame.

Marcel can also provide a deeper understanding of Will Percy's stoicism. Granting that ordeal in the form of great personal loss or sickness may provoke in some the response of the stoic, Marcel warns that the stoic is imprisoned within the self, a person who "bears himself—and that means above all he controls his interior life—as though he had no neighbors, as though he were concerned only with himself and had no responsibility towards anyone else" (*HV* 38). Hope and intersubjectivity depend upon and nourish one another: "hope is only possible on the level of the *us* . . . it does not exist on the level of the solitary ego, self-hypnotized and concentrating exclusively on individual aims" (*HV* 10).

Walker Percy must have found Marcel's "Sketch of a Phenomenology and a Metaphysic of Hope" particularly relevant to his situation, considering that his father's suicide probably resulted from despair. He had also lived sufficiently close to Will for enough years to recognize that his uncle found no help for his loneliness in Marcus Aurelius's "unassailable wintry kingdom" of self (*LL* 313). In his introduction to *Lanterns on the Levee*, Walker Percy certainly has this recognition, along with a warning against the yearning for doom toward which such stoicism may lead: "While granting the prescience of much of *Lanterns on the Levee's* pessimism, we must, I think, guard against a certain seductiveness which always attends the heralding of apocalypse, and we must not overlook some far less dramatic but perhaps equally significant counterforces" (*LL* xiv). Because Marcel acknowledges that "there can be no hope except when the temptation to despair exists," (*HV* 35) grounding his metaphysics of hope firmly in an understanding of the reality of despair, Percy must have found Marcel's argument in favor of hope both thought-provoking and healing, a much needed counterbalance to his uncle's stoic acceptance.

The defiant hope that Percy found in Marcel's concept of intersubjective love between individuals is powerfully embodied in the concrete world of the six novels he has given us to date. We might even suspect that Percy's concern with the interrelations of humankind was at least partly motivated by a cue in one of Marcel's observations: "The kind of writer who makes the mystery of the family palpable to us is always . . . the novelist rather than the historian of social institutions" (*MB* 1: 251). Percy sees his novelistic task as one of dealing with "the postmodern consciousness as he finds it and as he incarnates it in his own characters." He continues: "The psychical forces presently released in the postmodern consciousness open unlimited possibilities for both destruction and liberation, for an absolute loneliness or a rediscovery of community and reconciliation."[41] Marcel's concept of intersubjectivity promises that people who encounter each other as presences can create meaningful lives together. Percy emphasizes the hope to be found in intersubjective communion in his six novels.

Percy's first novel, *The Moviegoer* (1961), has at its center the developing intersubjective relationship between Binx Bolling and his aunt's stepdaughter, Kate Cutrer. Although Binx is embarked on a search for meaning, his life is totally without purpose until he recognizes Kate as "I myself" and takes her seriously as Marcel's "other," who knows him and with whom he can build a world. What is lacking in this novel, however, is a more fully rounded Kate, a character with whom Percy identifies but still fails to render as a complete "thou." The problem seems to lie in the first person point of view of the novel. Outside of the dramatic scenes in which Kate speaks for herself, we see Kate only as Binx sees her. And Binx himself, an elusive character fond of playing games, often prefers to see Kate as quite neurotic, probably because she is "onto" him, seeing through all his stratagems. Still, the basic requirements for intersubjective relationships are all present in Percy's first novel. More importantly, perhaps, the meaningless or moribund lives of the novel's characters emphasize the need for such relationships.

Percy's second novel, *The Last Gentleman* (1966), provides a larger canvas than *The Moviegoer*. We follow Will Barrett as he journeys from New York through the South, where he remembers the traumatic event of his father's suicide, and finally west to Santa Fe. Diffuse and episodic, *The Last Gentleman* has the honor of introducing Percy's most spiritually available protagonist. Although he suffers from fugues and spells of amnesia, Williston Bibb Barrett is an other-directed man, reaching out to members of the troubled Vaught family, always attempting to be of use to others. When Will Barrett's love, Kitty Vaught, becomes so caught up in her effort to be the perfect college coed that she becomes totally unavailable to Will, he follows her two brothers west and provides loving care for young Jamie in his last illness. After Jamie's death, Will offers himself to Sutter Vaught as someone who needs him, in an attempt to save Sutter from the suicide to which he is drawn. Marcel's concept of "invocation"—the call of one individual to another—is strongly evoked in the final scene of the novel.

In *Love in the Ruins* (1971), Percy moves his abstracted scientist, represented by Sutter Vaught in the previous novel, to the forefront in Dr. Thomas More. More has invented a "lapsometer" that will, he believes, solve the problems that have beset the modern individual ever since Descartes tore the *cogito* loose from the body, thus assuring that the individual would wander abstracted from the world and at a loss over how to live a life. Essentially, the lapso-meter is a mechanical device, a prophylactic substitute for individuals learning how to solve their own problems and to love each other. When Tom More finally spurns the demonic Art Immelmann in order to save his nurse, Ellen Oglethorpe, he makes a commitment to her that saves him. The intersubjective solution to Tom More's predicament, a spontaneous prayer that saves Ellen and himself from the devil, assumes greater efficacy to the extent that we recognize the novel's echoes of Marcel's thought.

The protagonist of *Lancelot* (1977), having lost all faith in his fellow man as a result of his wife's infidelity, completely rejects intersubjectivity. A bitter man, Lancelot Andrewes Lamar grows angrier in the course of telling his story, a dramatic monologue delivered to a silent John, the priest who visits him at the Center for Aberrant Behavior where Lance has been incarcerated since the murder, explosion, and fire at his ancestral home, Belle Isle, Louisiana. Lancelot embodies Marcel's idea of the damnation implicit in turning away from one's fellow creatures, and his plans for a fascist "New Order" are even more chilling than the narrative of his violent acts at Belle Isle. What hope there is in the novel is embodied in the mute but responsive John, who recommits himself to his faith as a result of listening to Lance's raving. Seeing the alternative to intersubjective love in the distorted mirror of Lancelot's tale, John can do nothing else. *Lancelot*, like *Love in the Ruins*, is Percy's attempt to show that Yeats's center has indeed not held in the modern world. The present age seems to offer only two alternatives: Lancelot's totalitarian New Order or John's intersubjective Christian love. The novel serves as a pivotal work for Percy, who returns in his next novel to the earlier theme of intersubjectivity as salvation for two people who can love each other.

The Second Coming (1980) reintroduces Will Barrett, twenty years older than he was in *The Last Gentleman*, now afflicted with total recall instead of amnesia, and determined to find out whether life is worth living and whether or not God exists. In a bizarrely funny episode, Will descends into a cave where he intends to remain until God declares Himself by giving Will a sign. But an abscessed tooth sends Will back into the world, and he falls out of the cave and into Allison Huger's greenhouse. The love that develops between Will and Allie, an escapee from a mental institution who is dedicated to beginning her life anew, ultimately saves them both. Percy's affirmation of the grace available in intersubjectivity, along with finely wrought scenes of the hunting trip Will Barrett took as a boy with his father, makes this novel his finest achievement. For the first time, Percy creates a female character who breathes—one who is as rounded, complex and intriguing as his male protagonist. Allie Huger thus provides a fitting "thou" for Will Barrett, who is determined to have it all, both Allie and God. Having struggled with the concept of intersubjectivity for more than twenty years, examining it from all angles and considering its opposite, Percy triumphs in his fifth novel by creating two individuals who come together in an affirmation of the power of hope and love.

In his most recent novel, *The Thanatos Syndrome* (1987), Percy returns to the public world of *Love in the Ruins*. Tom More returns to Feliciana parish to find it given over to death and other abstractions, a world in danger of fulfilling Lancelot's mad dreams of a New Order. In this novel, both adventure story and philosophical undertaking, two plot lines contribute to the implicit assertion that, ultimately, only intersubjective love can understand the individual and that all social engineers, who work from abstractions and generalizations, must be carefully watched lest they engineer a world in which it is imposible to live. Father Smith, the priest who heard More's confession in the epilogue of *Love in the Ruins*, moves to the forefront of this novel, where he becomes Percy's stand-in and Tom More's mentor. Without Father Smith's counsel, it is unlikely the good doctor would have been able to overthrow the powers of darkness represented by Drs. Bob Comeaux and John Van Dorn. The intersubjective relationship between the priest and Tom More, who no longer knows what he believes, offers hope at the end of the novel. In addition, Tom More's continuing work with his patients, to whom he listens as they name for him their unformulable selves, demonstrates Percy's continuing interest in the intersubjective nature of language.

Binx Bolling

From Spectator to Participant

Percy's first protagonist, John Bickerson Bolling, is a 29-year-old stocks and bonds broker living in a suburb of New Orleans without a clue as to how to live a life. Binx Bolling has created several stratagems ostensibly designed to discover a meaningful way to live, but ironically they prevent him from having an authentic encounter with others. He claims to take delight in making money—"for money is a great joy"—and in pursuing his secretaries, who are as interchangeable as the popular names they bear: Marcia, Linda and Sharon.[1] Binx is careful, however, to avoid committing himself to any of these women so that, failing to achieve real intimacy with him, the women eventually break off the relationship.[2] Although Binx takes great pains to convince himself and us that he is enjoying his life, he is actually living a life of despair. Percy says Binx "simply lived . . . a rather cool, detached exercise in cultivating different sensations. And his girlfriends, his business, his reading, were all a kind of playacting."[3]

In the crucial eight days of the novel's present, Binz moves from alienation and unavailability to a tentative communion with Kate Cutrer, the troubled stepdaughter of his formidable Aunt Emily. As Binx finally comes to recognize Kate in terms of Marcel's "other" with whom he can share his life, he moves from an inauthentic way of living to an authentic one, committed at least to Kate and prepared to be committed to other people. He also shifts from behaving largely as a spectator to living as a participant in being. Binx's sudden reversal near the end of the novel, his recognition of Kate as "I myself," and his somewhat Kierkegaardian leap into marriage with Kate are far less surprising if we look carefully at the developing intersubjectivity between Binx and Kate.[4]

At first introduced only as another of the "problems" that confront Binx, Kate Cutrer moves slowly to the forefront of the novel as her presence becomes increasingly and compellingly forced upon Binx's attention. Before he comes to see Kate as the other who needs him, much of Binx's life is either a shallow plot—"At four o'clock I decide it is not too early to set in motion my newest scheme conceived in the interests of money and love" (102)—or an amoral exercise in scientific method—"Tonight, Thursday night, I carry out a successful experiment in repetition" (79). Binx calculates and plans his life as if he were writing it instead of living it. Caught up in his various searches and impersonations, he is at first almost unaware of Kate except insofar as he has a duty to her as a member of his aunt's family and in the light of "this our old friendship" (63).

Through recollections in Percy's first person narrative, Binx reveals that he has devoted the last four years to living "the most ordinary life imaginable, a life without the old longings," in the most ordinary middle class suburb of New Orleans, Gentilly (9). On the day the novel opens, however, Binx has the unusual sense that he can overcome his self-effacing immersion in the quotidian and discover his true identity. As is often the case in Percy's novels, the startling clarity that suddenly results from apprehending the reality of physical objects in the world causes Binx to reawaken to the possibilities of life. Binx awakens from a dream of the Korean War, his attention riveted on ordinary objects on his dresser, a dawning recognition of the concrete reality of the physical world that he first experienced years ago in Korea as he lay wounded:

> My shoulder didn't hurt but it was pressed hard against the ground as if somebody sat on me. Six inches from my nose a dung beetle was scratching around under the leaves. As I watched, there awoke in me an immense curiosity. I was onto something. I vowed that if I ever got out of this fix, I would pursue the search. Naturally, as soon as I got home, I forgot all about it. But this morning when I got up, I dressed as usual and began as usual to put my belongings into my

pockets: wallet, notebook . . . pencil, keys, handkerchief, pocket slide rule. . . . They looked both unfamiliar and at the same time full of clues (10–11).

For much of the novel, the search for these clues absorbs Binx. He enjoys playing detective, ferreting out hints on how to live his life. He is particularly interested in finding out more about his father: "Any doings of my father, even his signature, is in the nature of a clue in my search" (71).[5] As for the Jews of whom he has become "acutely aware," Binx notes, "There is a clue here, but of what I cannot say"(88).

While he correctly apprehends clues, Binx makes the mistake of trying to perceive them and his life from the outside, from the standpoint of a scientific observer. His "searches" also show his effort to take an objective stance toward reality. Before the novel begins, Binx had attempted a "vertical search" for the meaning of life, but he abandoned it when he discovered about the scientific method what Kierkegaard discovered about Hegel's philosophy: "though the universe had been disposed of, I myself was left over. There I lay in my hotel room with my search over yet still obliged to draw one breath and then the next" (70). Binx therefore turns to this other search, one he names the horizontal. Nevertheless, he remains as cut off in his horizontal search as he was in the vertical because he adheres to the methodology of a scientist, watching those around him with the same kind of spectatorial fascination he once had for the dung beetle, but not participating in life with them.

For most of the novel, Binx clings to his objective-transcendent viewpoint. He assumes that he can look at his life from the outside, as if he were Descartes's disembodied *cogito*, cut off from the world it would know. Such objectivity, of course, is suitable to investigating an object, but is utterly inappropriate to learning about another person as subject. Kate, as we shall see, is aware of Binx's abstraction from his own life and from others. Binx's only possibility of ever integrating himself into the world lies in the approach of Gabriel Marcel: to open himself to the subjectivity of the other in love.

Walker Percy's indebtedness to Marcellian ideas is clear in this first novel. By the time he began work on *The Moviegoer*, Percy had already published a number of essays in which he discussed Marcel's concepts.[6] By scrupulously avoiding real encounters with others, Binx is really Marcel's *homo spectans*, a spectator, rather than *homo particeps*, a participant (*MB* 1: 157). Hiding behind his impersonations of movie stars and behind the experiments that he conducts in repetition and rotation, Binx stands apart from life, projecting his own emptiness onto the world and then solipsistically reading it back. Thus, we are skeptical when Binx declares, "For some time now the impression has been growing upon me that everyone is dead. It happens when I speak to people. In the middle of a sentence it will come over me: yes, beyond a doubt this is death" (99). Although the people he watches may indeed be moribund, Binx Bolling is not the most reliable of narrators. Chances are that not all those around Binx are as dead as he is, a condition that he himself suspects. For on several occasions, Binx refers to himself as a ghost, one who reads *Arabia Deserta*, and who lives in the contemporary desert of Gentilly. Kate confirms his suspicion when she tells him that he is "as cold as the grave" (83).

Marcel offers a relevant profile of what is likely to happen to a spectator like Binx: "The more we treat the world as spectacle, the more unintelligible must it necessarily seem from a metaphysical point of view, because the relation then established between us and the world is an intrinsically absurd one" (*BH* 19). Still worse, the spectator risks turning observation into such a rarefied activity that he loses his hold on reality:

> It may happen that I . . . turn myself into a pure spectator. But this change of front carries with it the risk that the whole may also tend to appear to me as a pure spectacle, perhaps even a spectacle lacking in sense. For the intelligent force . . . could perhaps only be grasped by me insofar as I was actively associated with it. A kind of rift then appears, either between me and the total, or, still more serious, between me and myself (*BH* 17).

Because of the rift that develops within Binx, he loses whatever *ontological* sense he may have had of having a body, of being incarnated. Thus, he often observes that he risks becoming a disembodied spirit: "There is a danger of slipping clean out of space and time. It is possible to become a ghost and not know whether one is in downtown Loews in Denver or suburban Bijou in Jacksonville" (75). And in considering the malaise that he sees all around him, Binx further dislocates himself by casting his self-analysis in the second person: "The world is lost to you, the world and the people in it, and there remains only you and the world and you no more able to be in the world than Banquo's ghost" (120). Having so little sense of his corporeal self, it is no wonder that Binx prefers not to drive his car: "The truth is I dislike cars. Whenever I drive a car, I have the feeling that I have become invisible" (11).

Unable to make sense of his world, Binx escapes to the movie theater, the appropriate analogue for his natural and self-willed tendency to engage in observation. "The fact is I am quite happy in a movie, even a bad movie," he tells us (7). Moviegoing is one stratagem that Binx uses to orient himself: while he is in the theater, all life is reduced to the image on the screen, his own eyes are interchangeable with the camera, and "real" life is temporarily suspended. Outside in the real world, Binx adopts the fictive world of the cinema, impersonating the gestures and expressions of famous screen stars who, like William Holden, seem to have a "peculiar reality" that he lacks (17).

Binx's moviegoing and his essential isolation from others illustrate his lack of the quality Marcel names *disponibilité*, availability. In "The Ego and Its Relation to Others," Marcel contrasts the individual who is available (*disponible*) to himself and to others, a person who has "an aptitude to give [him]self to anything which offers, and to bind [him]self by the gift" (*HV* 23) with the individual who is "occupied or cluttered up with himself" (*HV* 17). The self-centered person acts as if there were no others, mired in an ego which Marcel calls "the wound I bear within me" (*HV* 16). Binx Bolling resembles Marcel's unavailable person, burdened with himself and unaware that the self is after all "nothing but an empty void" (*HV* 16). Binx becomes a *poseur*, one who assumes roles in order to engage another person but who never approaches the "other" as a presence. In one of his more clearsighted moments, Binx admits that his life in Gentilly has been "the worst kind of self-deception" (18). He also confesses to his poor relations with others: "For years now I have had no friends. I spend my entire time working, making money, going to movies and seeking the company of women" (41).

Binx's posturing may be seen clearly in his attempted seduction of his current secretary, Sharon Kincaid. In his office on Friday morning, Binx decides to play his part as a movie star might: "It is possible to stand at the window, loosen my collar and rub the back of my neck like Dana Andrews" (105). Shortly thereafter, conscious of his every gesture, Binx enacts another role with the hope of seeing himself reflected back to himself as another of his idols, Rory Calhoun (106). Binx thus substitutes for his real self his impersonation of an actor who is himself adopting the identity of someone else. In this way, Binx conforms to Marcel's definition of the *poseur*:

> The *poseur* who seems only to be preoccupied with others is in reality entirely taken up with himself. Indeed, the person he is with only interests him insofar as he is likely to form a favorable picture of him which in turn he will receive back. The other person reflects him, returns to him this picture which he finds so enchanting. . . . From the moment that I become preoccupied about the effect I want to produce on the other person, my every act, word and attitude loses its authenticity (*HV* 17).

Moving a step further, Marcel argues that the *poseur* creates his own idea of the other for whom he is performing and that this "simulacrum" becomes a substitute for the real person because "the truth of the matter is that to pose is always to pose before oneself. . . . we might say that the other person is the provisional and as it were accessory medium, through which I can arrive at forming a certain image, or idol of myself" (*HV* 78).[7] So long as all the "others" whom he meets are reduced to simulacra by his posing, Binx does not have a chance of encountering them as presences.[8] Thus Binx shows by his behavior that he is Marcel's unavailable person, burdened with self, cut off from the human community.

In his isolation from others, Binx resembles his father more than he would care to admit. He is preoccupied with a photograph of his father and his two uncles which stands on the mantelpiece in Aunt Emily's house. He observes that his father "looks different from [his] brothers" who are "serene in their identities" (25).

Trying to read the clues in the photograph, Binx concludes only that his father's "eyes are alight with an expression I can't identify. . . . Beyond a doubt they are ironical" (25). Like his father, Binx feels separated from the other members of his father's family who, like Aunt Emily, believe in a stoical code of conduct. Never one to miss a chance to instruct Binx, Aunt Emily tells him, "In this world goodness is destined to be defeated. But a man must go down fighting. That is the victory" (54).[9]

Binx's father was a romantic who finally managed to achieve what Denis de Rougement argues every romantic searches for—death, and not just an ordinary death, but a romantic death off Crete "in the wine dark sea. . . . with a copy of *The Shropshire Lad* in his pocket" (25). Binx cannot believe in the romantic version of his family that is urged on him by Aunt Emily. Her stoicism combined with a romantic nostalgia for the bygone days of the ancestors (now raised to godlike status) are not acceptable to Binx. While his father's irony issued from an inability to find any ontological stance toward the world save a failed romanticism, Binx takes refuge in the objective-empirical approach of science.

Like the romantic, the scientist has difficulty re-entering the world of lived experience from a transcendent orbit. As Marcel argues, the ontological standpoint of the scientist is really impossible: "I cannot really stand aside from the universe, even in thought. Only by a meaningless pretense can I place myself at some vague point outside it" (*BH* 19). Binx fails to see any connection between his moviegoing romanticism, his own desire to imitate the "gestural perfection" of Hollywood's leading men, and the romanticism that led to his father's death in World War II. Binx does, however, acknowledge that he was once somewhat of a romantic himself. Of the letters that he wrote during the Korean War, he remarks: "A regular young Rupert Brooke was I, '—full of expectancy.' Oh the crap that lies lurking in the English soul. Somewhere it, the English soul, received an injection of romanticism that nearly killed it. That's what killed my father, English romanticism, that and 1930 science" (88). Still thinking about his father, Binx goes on to make a connection between the romantic and scientific views of reality.[10] The romantic looks at life from a transcendent remove while the scientist studies the world from a position above it. Binx needs to see this similarity in order to comprehend the futility of both his vertical and horizontal searches. Accordingly, Binx instructs himself: "Explore connection between romanticism and scientific objectivity. Does a scientifically minded person become a romantic because he is a left-over from his own science?" (88). The connection here expressed in question form is the one that Binx badly needs to make before he can acquire an understanding of life from *within* the living of it. His external observations only serve to distance him further from life.[11]

Concealed behind his observatorial distance and his impersonations, and caught up in his repetitions and rotations, Binx does not genuinely encounter his secretaries but rather meets them as a young well-to-do man on the make, imitating the gestures of movie stars. His relationship with Kate Cutrer, however, is radically different. When he is with her, Binx drops his impersonations and is himself. Thus he often "encounters" Kate in Marcel's sense of the word: "To encounter someone is not merely to cross his path but to be, for the moment at least, near to or with him. . . . it means being a *co-presence*."[12] The shared likeness entailed in this co-presence, so important in Percy's rendering of intersubjectivity, appears the first time Binx and Kate are alone together in the basement of the Cutrer house. Kate tells Binx that he is not a Bolling, but rather, "You're like me, but worse. Much worse" (43). She speaks a truth that Binx only comes to see in the novel's climax on Ash Wednesday. Dropping all pretenses when he is with Kate, Binx simply talks with her, and Kate's responses indicate that she understands him.

Binx and Kate have known each other from childhood, and perhaps they have always been alike. Like Binx, Kate also hides behind impersonations, having tried to become a "joyful and creative person" in order to please her psychiatrist, Merle Mink (115). Determined to abandon her role-playing, Kate tells Binx how hard she tried to impersonate herself: "There were days when I would come in as nervous as an actress and there were moments when I succeeded—in being myself and brilliantly (look at me, Merle, I'm doing it!), so brilliantly that I think he loved me" (114). Binx and Kate are also similar to the extent that they are wayfarers. On the first morning of the novel, Binx awakens to the possibility of a search, and midway through the novel, anticipating Binx, Kate makes an important discovery. During a therapy session with Dr. Minx, she suddenly realizes that she is free, that she no longer has to try to please Merle by fulfilling his expectations of her.

The novel provides slowly accumulating evidence that Binx and Kate have confided in each other for years. It is clear from her conversations with Binx that she has been privy to all his little searches, researches and experiments. For example, she accompanies Binx to the movies three times, fully recognizing their significance for him. After they see *Panic in the Streets*, which was filmed in New Orleans, Kate shows that she understands Binx's concept of "certification." Looking around the neighborhood when they emerge from the theater, Kate says, "Yes, it is certified now," confirming Binx's contention that when one sees one's own city in a movie, the place is made real, whereas normal familiarity with an area tends to cause a place to lose its reality.

Kate also perceives the importance of ritual in Binx's behavior. After she breaks her engagement to Walter Wade, Kate goes with Binx to see a Western, playing in a theater on Freret Street, where Binx had seen *The Oxbow Incident* years earlier. Binx is conducting a little experiment in the vitality of recurrence; and he is not disappointed, since he notices the same sensations that he experienced 14 years earlier: "There we sat, I in the same seat I think, and afterwards came out into the smell of privet. Camphor berries popped underfoot on the same section of broken pavement" (79). Yet what we especially notice is not the success of Binx's repetition but Kate's awareness that he has tried to cultivate it, which is apparent in her question after they leave the theater and walk through the dark campus: "Is this part of the repetition?" (81). And when Binx dissembles by saying that it is not, Kate persists with another question, "Part of the search?" Clearly, Kate has insight into the function of Binx's spectatorial way of being, and she is no doubt willing to indulge him because, to a considerable extent, his ways are identical with her own.

At this stage, of course, it is not surprising that Binx cannot validate Kate's insights. Considering himself inaccessible to her analysis, he deliberately tries to discredit her power of perception generally:

> [Kate] can only believe I am serious in her own fashion of being
> serious: as an antic sort of seriousness, which is not seriousness at all
> but despair masquerading as seriousness. I would as soon not speak
> to her of such things, since she is bound to understand it as a
> cultivated eccentricity, like the eccentricity of the roommate she used
> to talk about: "A curious girl, BoBo. Do you know what she like to
> do? Collect iron deer. She located every iron deer in Westchester
> County and once a month she'd religiously make her rounds and pay
> them a visit" (82).

Becoming irritable with Kate's effort to find out which of his
experiments they are conducting, Binx nevertheless admits that he
does "for a fact sound like BoBo and her goddam iron deer" (82).
In Kate's playing back to him her understanding of his behavior,
Binx entertains the absurdity of continually seeking out repetitions
and rotations.

That Kate understands and identifies with Binx becomes apparent
as she continues her interrogation. When she asks him about the
vertical search, Binx defines it for her: "If you walk in the front door
of the laboratory, you undertake the vertical search. You have a
specimen, a cubic centimeter of water or a frog or a pinch of salt or a
star. . . . As you get deeper into the search, you unify. You understand more and more specimens by fewer and fewer formulae" (82).
Yet it is Kate who summarizes the risk to the scientific generalizer of
becoming lost in abstraction: "And the danger is of becoming no one
nowhere" (83). This fear of losing specific individual reality constantly
troubles Binx, helping to explain why he needs to speak to the ticket
seller when he goes to the movies: "If I did not talk to the theater
owner or the ticket seller, I should be lost, cut loose metaphysically
speaking. I should be seeing one copy of a film which might be shown
anywhere and at any time" (75). Kate's phrase "no one nowhere" is
the corollary of Binx's "anywhere and at any time," and both echo
Marcel's explanation of the peril of abstraction:

> In abstracting myself from given circumstance, from the empirical
> self, from the situation in which I find myself, I run the risk of
> escaping into a real never-never or no-man's-land—into what must
> be called a *nowhere*, though it is a nowhere that I illegitimately
> transform into a privileged place, a high sanctuary, a kind of Olym-
> pus of the spirit (*MB* 1: 164).

That Kate further realizes the effect of abstracting from reality is clear when she dares to suggest that Binx may be "overlooking something, the most obvious thing of all. And you would not know it if you fell over it" (83). Although Binx cannot persuade Kate to tell him what she means, it is apparently Kate herself who is being overlooked. Her immediate actions thereafter suggest that love is what she dares not name when, on the bus, she becomes affectionate, locking her arms around Binx's waist and kissing him. Even after this physical demonstration of her understanding and empathy, Binx continues to be unable to see her as the "other" whom he could love. Still, Marcel's intersubjective naming process is clearly underway, establishing the foreground for Binx and Kate to conceive themselves as "I" and "thou."

Perhaps the first scene where we see decidedly that Binx and Kate are somehow in league with each other, comrades who share a secret apart from "the others," takes place at Aunt Emily's house. Binx has just returned from his weekend outing with Sharon at the Smith's fishing camp to be greeted with the bad news that Kate has taken too many nembutals the night before. Aunt Emily dispatches Binx to take care of Kate, and the two seat themselves in the dark mezzanine of the Cutrer house, actually and symbolically separated from the rest of the family. Binx remarks, "The view of the house, the hall and the dining room below, seems at once privileged and strange" (175). Kate, wrestling with the problem of whether or not she can figure out a way to live, cannot cope with the ordinary conversation at the table. Throughout the mezzanine scene, Binx and Kate's conversation is interspersed with the table talk below them, a reprise of the sort of talk on the previous night that raised Kate to the point of exhilaration from which she fell. While below them in the dining room Sam Yerger entertains the company, Kate tells Binx that she hadn't tried to commit suicide the night before. She explains that she simply wanted to break off "dead center" because everything seemed "so no 'count somehow" (181). Although Binx does not comment, Kate's observation that nothing in life seems worthwhile must strike a familiar chord with Binx, inasmuch as that very morning he had told his mother that in Korea he felt that "nothing seemed worth doing except something I couldn't even remember" (158).

Situated as they are in a kind of no-man's-land between the ground floor and the second, Kate and Binx share the experience of feeling the emptiness of life and the anxiety that arises in response to that knowledge, while below them "the others," who don't seem to have any problem coinciding with themselves, carry on in the familiar ways of those at Aunt Emily's dinners. In this scene, a growing intersubjective bond develops between Kate and Binx as she confides to him her own desperation. In naming her alienation for Binx, Kate makes it possible for him to be able to name his own despair.[13] Moreover, Kate now responds to the "proposal" Binx made two nights earlier at the bus stop in front of his home. "I thought about your proposal and it seemed to me that it might be possible after all" (178), says Kate, while looking down into the dining room "like a theater-goer in the balcony" (177).

Binx and Kate are set apart from the others by these bits of knowledge they share. Binx knows, for instance, that the accident that killed her first fiancé, Lyell Lovell, did not devastate Kate. Instead, as she says, "It gave me my life. That's my secret, just as the war is your secret" (58). In the midst of loss, both Kate and Binx are survivors. Kate has survived the deaths of her mother and fiancé; Binx has survived the deaths of his brother, father and those in the Korean War. Their secret of loss, of shared deprivation, falls into Marcel's category of the deep secret, which he describes as "a really incommunicable experience—generally a painful one—about which the initiated feel that others, who did not share it in the flesh, have no right to speak" (*MB* 1: 223). The centrality of the shared secret Marcel calls "the mainspring of intersubjectivity" (*MB* 1: 219). Both Kate and Binx are aware of living in the certain light of their own deaths.

Although Binx is not quite aware of it, the increasing intersubjectivity between him and Kate largely accounts for his willingness to take her with him on a business trip to Chicago by train. Kate's growing dependence on Binx is clear; she desires to be with him because "I am never too bad with you" (192). On the train, Kate continues to inaugurate the possibility of an intersubjective relationship with Binx by naming her own sense of the abyss and nothingness within her. Gradually, Binx begins to see his own situation mirrored in Kate's, as the simile he uses to describe the way they sit in Kate's compartment suggests: "We hunch up knee to knee and nose to nose like the two devils on the Rorschach card" (192). Binx's use of the word "devils" is critical here, not because it suggests that their escapade is sinful but because it implies that they may both be damned unless they discover their love for each other. And obviously the Rorschach simile insists that Binx and Kate are mirror images of each other, the required intersubjective presence of "I" and "thou."

After consuming a number of nembutals, Kate again tells Binx "You're like me"; she then explains that she cannot marry him unless he changes (193). Kate accuses Binx of seeing the possibility of their marrying as just "another one of [his] ingenious little researches" (193). If their marrige is to be only another of Binx's experiments, Kate realizes that she would be reduced to a specimen, and she would suffer the radical loss of being that being a specimen, an example of some "thing," not an individual, produces.[14] Having accepted her own freedom and her absolute unformulability— "a person does not have to *be* this or *be* that or be anything, not even oneself. One is free"—Kate must guard against any potential attempt by Binx to reduce her to formula, a little wife for "hubby" (114). There must be no more games between them; they must be open and truthful: "Let us not deceive one another," Kate implores (193).

Kate is quite clear in what she needs from Binx if they are to make a life together: she needs to be told what to do so that she will not lose her grasp on reality. Kate demonstrates by her request the enormous stride she has taken—from faith in theories of how to be (Merle Mink's "joyous and creative person") to faith in a person. Marcel argues that true belief is always belief in another person, a "thou": "Belief in the strong sense of the term—not in the sense of believing that, i.e. assuming that—is always belief in a *thou*, i.e. in a reality, whether personal or suprapersonal, which is able to be invoked" (*CF* 169). Unable to believe in God, Kate is still a religious person, and she knows that she trusts Binx, whom she compares to God: "You are the unmoved mover. You don't need God or anyone else—no credit to you unless it is a credit to be the most self-centered person alive. I don't know whether I love you, but I believe in you and I will do what you tell me" (197). Kate names both her belief in Binx and Binx's self-centeredness, his unavailability to others.

That Binx is beginning to respond to Kate's overtures is apparent in his frequent references to her eyes. There are more than ten descriptions of Kate's eyes during the train trip to Chicago. For example, Binx notes: "In celebration of Mardi Gras, she has made up her eyes with a sparkle of mascara and now she looks up at me with a black spiky look" (184–85); "I feel her eyes on my face" (187); "Her black spiky eyes fall full upon me, but not quite seeing, I think" (198). Unlike Sartre, who saw in the look of the other a hostile threat and shame at being reduced to an object, Percy believes that what is revealed to the self when another person looks at me is "literally my unspeakableness (unformulability)."[15] And whereas Sartre always presents the other as a threat to one's being, Percy insists that the other peson may also be one's salvation:

> A look can only be an aggression or a communion, nothing else. . . . In the exchange of stares everything is at stake. *L'enfer c'est autrui.* But so is heaven. . . . The Thou is the knower, the namer, the co-inspector with me of the common thing and the authority for its name. Whatever devious constitution of self I have been able to arrive at, whatever my "self-system," my impersonation, it melts away before the steady gaze of another.[16]

With her eyes constantly on Binx, Kate makes it difficult for him to continue to hide behind the impersonations that he regularly assumes. By naming the void within her, Kate likewise makes it possible for Binx to acknowledge his own "howling void" (202) and to commit himself to her. Consequently, their relationship verges on the creative vow endorsed by Marcel: "If you reveal yourself to me, you will give me the strength to consecrate myself to you" (*HV* 117).

Yet when Binx and Kate attempt to make love for the first time, taking refuge in their bodies, trying to find the "real thing," which Kate thinks must be sex, the experiment fails (199). Binx describes their failure:

> We did very badly and almost did not do at all. Flesh poor flesh failed us. The burden was too great and flesh poor flesh, neither hallowed by sacrament nor despised by spirit . . . but until this moment seen

through and canceled, rendered null by the cold and fishy eye of the
malaise—flesh poor flesh now at this moment summoned all at once
to be all and everything, end all and be all, the last and only
hope—quails and fails (200).

Both Kate and Binx have been so abstracted from their proper
ontological status as incarnated beings that when they try to fall
back on their bodies, to seal their tentative commitment by making
love, flesh—unaccustomed as it has become to being inhabited—
fails them, and they cannot consummate their incipient love. Part of
the problem seems to be their terror: "The truth is I was frightened
half to death by her bold . . . carrying on. . . . Kate too was scared.
We shook like leaves" (200). But the fact that they share this fear is a
potentially encouraging sign, a prefatory indication that they care
more about each other than they have admitted and more than mere
casual sex will allow.

That Binx is beginning to understand something of who Kate is,
how alike they are, becomes evident only after they arrive in
Chicago, where they reverse their roles from the train. Now it is
Binx who is lost and disoriented, who needs Kate to take care of
him, because he feels himself in danger of becoming "No one and
Nowhere" (99), the very person that Kate had previously named.
His feeling of helplessness, combined with Kate's competence,
permits Binx all at once to see Kate as he has never seen her before,
as they sit in a small bar in the Loop: "There I see her plain, see plain
for the first time since I lay wounded in a ditch and watched an
Oriental finch scratching around in the leaves—a quiet little body
she is, a tough little city Celt; no, more of a Rachel really, a dark
little Rachel bound home to Brooklyn on the IRT" (206). Although
Kate is her own unformulable self and not Rachel, the important
point to notice here is that Binx earlier identified himself with the
Jews, seeing in them his exile. Here he sees Kate as a Jew, alienated
and in exile, and therefore like him. Nevertheless, Binx does not
become fully conscious that they are both metaphorically wandering Jews, in exile, until they have returned home to New Orleans.

Binx's complete recognition of Kate as "I myself" occurs rapidly
after their return. After his aunt denounces him for betraying her by
taking advantage of Kate, Binx waits for Kate to join him in the

playground.[17] He sits on the "ocean wave," a merry-go-round which symbolically represents his future should he not reach out to another human being. Becoming desperate, thinking that he has lost Kate because Aunt Emily has convinced her that he is a cad, and consumed with desire, Binx calls his secretary, Sharon, because he must have someone: "I've got to find her. . . . It is certain now that my aunt is right and that Kate knows it and that nothing is left but Sharon" (229).

So desperate is Binx that when he gets Sharon's roommate, Joyce, he quickly turns on the charm, wheedling and flirting with Joyce to the extent that even he cannot stand to pay attention to what he is saying: "Old confederate Marlon Brando—a reedy insinuating voice, full of winks and leers and above all pleased with itself. What a shock. On and on it goes" (230). And as the flirtation continues, the merry-go-round keeps time to the conversation: "Round and round goes the ocean wave screeching out its Petrouchka music *iii-oorrr iii-oorrr* and now belling out so far that the inner bumper catches the pole and slings around in a spurt so outrageously past all outrage that the children embrace the iron struts for dear life" (230). The implication is that Binx himself is in the precarious position of the children on the merry-go-round, about to fall prey to the game playing and inauthenticity that have marked his life in Gentilly.

But then Kate arrives to save him from returning to his desperately alienated, spectator self:

> A watery sunlight breaks through the smoke of the Chef and turns the sky yellow. Elysian Fields glistens like a vat of sulfur; the playground looks as if it alone had survived the end of the world. At last I spy Kate; her stiff little Plymouth comes nosing into my bus stop. There she sits like a bomber pilot, resting on her wheel and looking sideways at the children and not seeing, and she could be I myself, sooty eyed and nowhere (231).

Kate's having kept her word to come to Binx if he would wait, and his conscious understanding that Kate is *like him*, lead to his sudden apprehension of what Kate really means to him. Thus he abruptly asks Joyce, who has just invited him to a party, "May I bring along my own fiancée, Kate Cutrer?" (231). In this question he seals his commitment to Kate by publicly naming her as his own.[18]

Binx demonstrates one of the ways in which Marcel says the mystery of commitment can occur:

> All fidelity is based on a certain relation which is felt to be inalterable, and therefore on an assurance which cannot be fleeting. Inspiration, the bolt from the blue, are limiting-cases which are ultimately not very much more mysterious than any others; they focus the mystery of commitment on a privileged, decisive moment (*CF* 164).

Binx's privileged moment of grace, his "bolt from the blue," allows him to see the individual who has been right in front of him all along, Kate Cutrer, a young woman who understands and needs him as much as he needs her. When Binx recognizes Kate as a subject, "I myself," rather than an object, he immediately experiences a surge of the kind of hope that Marcel describes as "a spring . . . the leaping of a gulf" (*BH* 79). Having recognized Kate, Binx questions his despair, asking, "Is it possible that—it is not too late?" (231). Binx possesses a lucid vision at this moment: he must choose between life that resembles the ocean wave, its very sounds, "*iii-oorrr iii-oorrr*," reminding the reader of Kierkegaard's "either-or," and a life committed to Kate, who loves him and needs him. In an instant he chooses.

Binx actually attains a multilevel commitment. Because he now takes responsibility for Kate, he can thereby commit himself to others who might also need him. Sitting in Kate's car, Binx thinks of the answer that he will give his Aunt Emily about what he intends to do with his life: "There is only one thing I can do: listen to people, see how they stick themselves into the world, hand them along a ways in their dark journey and be handed along, and for good and selfish reasons" (233). Through his commitment to Kate, Binx rejoins the human community. Although he still does not have all the answers for which he was searching, his words here indicate that he will be more available to his fellow beings in the future, that his intention now is to be a participant as well as a spectator. In addition to observing his fellow beings, he will attempt to "hand them along a ways in their dark journey": and to accept their help when he needs it. Binx has become Marcel's *homo viator*.[19]

As Kate and Binx watch a middle-class black man enter the church across the street, apparently to receive the mark of Ash Wednesday, Kate tells Binx, "The only time I'm not frightened is when I'm with you. You'll have to be with me a great deal" (234). Binx promises Kate that he will be with her and that he will tell her what to do. He then pledges his fidelity to Kate by making a secular communion: "[Kate] has started plucking at her thumb in earnest, tearing away little shards of flesh. I take her hand and kiss the blood" (234).

The change in Binx may be observed in the manner in which he describes the black man as he leaves the church. Binx observes what the man *does*, but he does not presume to tell the reader who the man *is* or why he has come. Binx's new refusal to draw conclusions based on observation indicates his acceptance of ambiguity, his willingness to be a part of life without assuming that he can figure it out. This acceptance marks Binx's new life of intersubjectivity with Kate. Now humbler, more aware of his own place in the world, his own unformulability, Binx reports what he sees and distinguishes what he sees from what he can guess at but cannot possibly *know*:

> The Negro has already come outside. His forehead is an ambiguous sienna color and pied: it is impossible to be sure that he received ashes. . . . I watch him closely in the rear-view mirror. It is impossible to say why he is here. Is it part and parcel of the complex business of coming up in the world? Or is it because he believes that God himself is present here at the corner of Elysian Fields and Bons Enfants? Or is he here for both reasons: through some dim dazzling trick of grace, coming for the one and receiving the other as God's own importunate bonus?
> It is impossible to say (234–35).

Binx's refusal even to draw the conclusion that the man has received ashes demonstrates his new unwillingness to proclaim who another individual is. Having seen his own limitations mirrored in Kate's eyes, having been given by grace the gift of realizing that he cannot name himself but that with Kate as the other he may discover who he 'is, Binx withholds judgment and admits the limitations of the objective-empirical approach to reveal anything about being.

These two paragraphs that conclude the novel proper stand in marked contrast to the opening paragraph of the first chapter in which Binx announces in a voice full of authority and self-satisfaction that he has received a note from his aunt asking him to lunch. "I know what this means," he tells the reader and proceeds to explain (3). On Ash Wednesday, a different and less decisive Binx admits that observation can tell him what the churchgoer looks like and what his gestures are, but not who he is or why he is there. Three times Binx admits, "It is impossible to say" (235). No longer the detached spectator, Binx is humble before Being, a participant who will accept all the ambiguities of the situation that is now his own.

The Epilogue, set somewhat more than a year later, gives every evidence that Binx has abandoned his role-playing, that he has become available to his family, and that he is now a full participant in life. He has assumed care of his half-brothers and sisters, along with full responsibility for Kate. The day Lonnie dies Binx makes good his Ash Wednesday promise to help his fellow creatures "along a ways in their dark journey." No longer self-absorbed and isolated, Binx brings his younger siblings a message from Lonnie. Unlike his Aunt Emily, who brought him the news of his brother Scott's death with the accompanying burden, "Now it's all up to you" (4), Binx names Lonnie's love for the children: "He wouldn't want you to be sad. He told me to give you a kiss and tell you that he loved you" (230).[20]

Binx's return to the Catholic Church is also implied in his response to his brother Donice, who asks if Lonnie will be crippled when he arises on the Last Day. Binx assures Donice that Lonnie's resurrected body will be sound, that he will be able to water ski. Although Binx refuses to comment on his religious beliefs because "I am a member of my mother's family after all and so naturally shy away from the subject of religion," there is every reason to believe that Binx speaks from the conviction of faith and that he now believes in the resurrection of the body (237).[21]

In continuing to care for Kate, Binx responds to the call from a thou who needs him desperately. He therefore does for Kate what he could not do for his father. After his brother Scott died, his father came to expect everything from his remaining son. In Chicago with Kate, Binx remembers another trip to that city with his father, several years after Scott died. He recalls standing in front of a tableau of Stone Age Man, "father mother and child crouched around an artificial ember" in the Field Museum:

> Feeling my father's eye on me, I turned and saw what he required of me—very special father and son we were that summer, he staking his everything this time on a perfect comradeship—and I, seeing in his eyes the terrible request, requiring from me his very life; I, through a child's cool perversity or some atavistic recoil from an intimacy too intimate, turned him down, turned away, refused him what I knew I could not give (204).

The young Binx, faced with the terrible burden of being everything to his father, even the reason for his father's continuing to live, instinctively recoiled from such a request.[22] But the mature Binx, who has wandered until he is 30, avoiding intimacy and cut off from love, gives Kate what he could not offer his father, a reason *to be*. He shows his love for Kate by responding to her request to be told what to do, to name her life so that she can live it.

The final scene also illustrates Binx's fulfilling exactly what Kate has asked. So that he can stay with his brothers and sisters, Binx sends Kate on an errand to pick up some government bonds at his office, telling her step by step just what she must do. Then, as a final gesture that reminds her of his fidelity, he picks a jasmine flower and gives it to her to hold. Realizing that Binx gives her himself along with the flower, Kate rehearses exactly how she will sit on the bus:

> "I'm going to sit next to the window on the Lake side and put the cape jasmine in my lap?"
> "That's right."
> "And you'll be thinking of me just that way?"
> "That's right" (242).

Here, as in Marcel's "The Ego and Its Relation to Others," the flower Binx gives Kate serves as a symbol of the real gift, which is the gift of self. By telling Kate that he will think of her with the flower, picture her sitting on the bus, Binx helps Kate find the courage she needs to undertake the errand. The significant difference in their status is made plain when Kate expresses her fear of something going wrong. Binx reassures her that if the errand becomes too much for her, she can simply, "Get off and walk home" (241). It is now clear that Kate has a home to go to, a refuge from the world that previously threatened to engulf her.

Will Barrett

Man for Others

Percy's protagonist in *The Last Gentleman*, Williston Bibb Barrett, a 25-year-old Southerner living in New York, is an unusual young man beset with a number of problems, some specific to his "condition," others indicative of the modern predicament of humankind. Like Binx Bolling, Will Barrett is a watcher and a waiter who thinks that he needs advice from experts in order to know how to live.[1] He has a collection of symptoms which remove him from ordinary experience: he is deaf in one ear, prone to amnesia and fugue states, and afflicted with a jerking knee that he must often physically restrain. Some of Will's difficulties issue directly from his father's suicide, resulting in a condition close to hysterical amnesia.[2] As the novel opens, Will has just broken off intensive therapy with Dr. Gamow, "fifty-five minutes a day, five days a week, for . . . five years."[3]

A dropout from Princeton where he was miserable trying to be happy—"what a sad business it was for him, this business of being a youth at college" (14)—Barrett lives like an exile in New York, working nights as a "humidification engineer" at Macy's and living at the YMCA. Cut off from himself and others, Will Barrett seems to be haunted by his own existence. He feels "left over" without knowing what he is left over from. He has no sense of self to remind him of who he is or of what he must do. Thus he qualifies as Percy and Marcel's *homo viator*, but he is unaware that he is a wayfarer, and ignorant of the Christian message of how to make sense of his ontological position in the world.[4] A representative of post-Christian man, Barrett is, as Sutter Vaught records in his notebook, "in favor of the World's Great Religions" (354), in the same way that he attends to working out in order to preserve his physical health. Hence, although Will "watches and waits," he does not know what he is watching and waiting for. Instead, like modern humankind in general, he puts faith in the principles of science (and of psychotherapy). After he breaks off therapy with Dr. Gamow, Will sets forth into the world determined to put what he has learned to good use, declaring: "I shall engineer the future of my life according to the scientific principles and the self-knowledge I have so arduously gained from five years of analysis" (41).

Will Barrett's determination to approach the world as an observer with a set of definitive principles identifies him, like Binx Bolling, as Marcel's observer. Will's desire "to know without being known" (170) precludes attaining intersubjectivity, for it is only through participation in being and the affirmation of self that he can, through the other, discover his identity.[5] So long as Will continues to place his faith in an objective approach to being, he will stand outside the world as its knower, imitating an English detective who is "perfectly disguised or perfectly hidden, holed up maybe in the woods of Somerset, actually hiding for days at a time in a burrow of ingenious construction" (161).

Will Barrett's salvation comes from an unlikely source—the Southern family Vaught—in a way that Percy believes may afford accessibility to being.[6] Dr. Gamow's diagnosis that Will is "having difficulty relating to other people in a meaningful way" is correct (39). But the doctor's psychoanalytic jargon, used to describe Will's condition and to recommend that he enter group therapy, reduces Will's individual problem to one which is representative of a class of people who have trouble "relating." What Will actually needs, however, are individuals with whom to share a world that is named more concretely. Dr. Gamow has the right message, but he is the wrong messenger.[7]

Instead of joining group therapy as Dr. Gamow recommends, Will enters the circle of the troubled Vaught family, which is caught up in the ordeal of 16-year-old Jamie's approaching death from leukemia. Will Barrett's chance encounter with the Vaughts becomes a providential event because he learns more from direct participation with the Vaughts than he could from the self-concealing experiences of Dr. Gamow's group therapy. The way for Will to recover himself and to find out about love is in a family, an actual network of people rather than an artificial group of patients, where intersubjectivity, though sought, is almost certain to remain elusive. Will uses his "amiable Southern radar" to reach out to the Vaughts; he joins them, makes love available to them, and opens the possibility of an intersubjective experience of the world to Jamie Vaught, his sister Kitty and his elder brother Sutter.

The Last Gentleman is replete with Will Barrett's attempts to establish intersubjective relationships with others. The first half of the novel centers on the failure of Will's love affair with Kitty Vaught. The second half develops his relationship with Kitty's brother Sutter, a scientist who lives in despair because he cannot return from his transcendent sphere to the immanent world. Joining the two halves of the novel is Will's search for intersubjectivity.

Although Will is badly in need of another person to love, his problem does not really have much to do with his ability to fit into groups. So much of a chameleon is Will that when he is with a group of Ohioans, he takes on their mannerisms and their pronunciation: "In short, he became an Ohioan and for several weeks walked like a cat with his toes pointed in, drank beer, forgot the old honorable quarrels of the South" (21). Earlier, when Will had been at Princeton, he had done all the right things to fit in: "He did very well in his studies, joined a good club, made the boxing team, but funked it nevertheless" (13). Will "funked it" because he had no sense of self. Accordingly, his problem in adapting to people is not that he is *not* like them but that he is *so* like them that he tends to become invisible. He therefore never gets to know others, cannot name a world with them, cannot find the special Marcellian "other" with whom to build a life of shared definitions.

Because he is so often out of touch with his own being, Will is usually all openness and availability, which makes him in some ways the most appealing of Percy's protagonists. Lost and wacky, he is nevertheless kindhearted and well-intentioned; and although he exists in a total state of confusion, he is a welcome relief from those protagonists who look endlessly within. Perhaps Will's forgetfulness and resultant availability are some of what Percy had in mind when citing Kierkegaard's admonition, "If a man cannot forget, he will never amount to much," which appears in the first epigraph to the novel. Will's nervous condition and amnesia cause the loss of self that leads to his being a model of what David Riesman defines as an other-directed individual.[8] While Will is pathologically more ill than Percy's other protagonists, he is also somewhat of a holy innocent through whom God's love can shine, the one who most demonstrates Marcel's *disponibilité*, openness and spiritual availability to those who need him.[9]

When Will first meets Jamie Vaught, he immediately senses that the boy is dying, and he senses it even more deeply when the two travel south in the Trav-L-Aire. Yet rather than deserting Jamie, Will draws closer to him, as if he somehow knows that his own problems have something to do with death and that, through the experience of Jamie's death, he might acquire an insightful vantage on the trauma of his father's suicide. At first, Percy treats the death of Will's father somewhat marginally and ambiguously:

> At the end of the summer his father died. Though his death was sudden, people were less surprised than they might have been since it was well known that in this particular family the men died young, after short tense honorable lives, and the women lived another fifty years (16–17).

Except for the confounding clause, "In the end he was killed by his own irony and sadness and by the strain of living out an ordinary day in a perfect dance of honor," Percy offers no further intimation for some time that Will's father took his own life (10). But as Will travels farther south, following the Vaught family, memories of the last night he spent with his father return periodically in a series of dreams and flashbacks, until he finally remembers the whole sequence of events.[10]

The various physical manifestations of Will's nervous condition can be traced to the fact that he was present when his father killed himself, the deafness in his right ear resulting from the concussion of the shotgun blast, his fugue states resulting from not being able to remember what happened. As a medical doctor, Percy has a very specific condition in mind here, although he does not name it. Will Barrett's "nervous condition" best fits the description of Psychogenic Fugue given in the American Psychiatric Association's

Diagnostic and Statistical Manual of Disorders. Psychogenic Fugue occurs most commonly in wartime or in the wake of natural disasters, but it also manifests itself in travel and more purposeful action than the confused wandering that accompanies Psychogenic Amnesia.[11] We should therefore note that, while Will sometimes loses his bearings as he follows the Vaught family around the country, there is always a purpose to his traveling. For example, Will deliberately pursues Sutter Vaught because he senses that Sutter may be able to help him. Will's travels also lead him to his hometown of Ithaca, where he stands in front of his boyhood home and finally remembers the night his father shot himself.

Partly because he has such a tenuous hold on his own life, Will resorts to mechanical means to recover the physical world of objects from the "ravenous particles" that he sees obscuring them (26). He buys a $1,900 Tetzlar telescope with which he hopes to "penetrate to the heart of things" (29). Ultimately, of course, the objective-empirical way of looking at the world only serves to abstract Will further from his own life, but the telescope does afford common ground for Will and young Jamie Vaught. Having no birthday gift for Jamie, Will gives him the telescope, enabling Jamie to see the world as Will has seen it, a world outside his hospital window: "He must watch the tugs on the river, the roller coaster at Palisades Park, the tollhouse on the George Washington Bridge. . . . . Now it was Jamie who became the technician, focusing on some bit of New Jersey and leaning away to let the doctors look" (76–77).

What Will really shares with Jamie is not the telescope but himself and a world that they can both observe and name. Later, when Will journeys south as Jamie's companion in the Trav-L-Aire, an intersubjective world opens between them:

> [Will] unlimbered the telescope and watched a fifty-foot Chris-Craft beat up the windy Intercoastal. A man sat in the stern reading the *Wall Street Journal*. . . . He called Jamie over. "Look how he pops his jaw and crosses his legs with the crease of his britches pulled out of the way."
>
> "Yes," said Jamie, registering and savoring what the engineer registered and savored. *Yes, you and I know something the man in the Chris-Craft will never know* (162).

This crucial passage shows how the world named is the world shared. Jamie takes real pleasure in seeing what Will sees as Will names it for him. According to Percy, naming provides the basis of intersubjectivity, because naming affirms the being of the namer, the hearer and the object, "an act the very essence of which is an 'is-saying,' an affirming of the thing to be what it is for both of us."[12] Realizing that he is creating a world for Jamie, Will meditates on the wonder of the affirmation of being that such naming provides: *"Yes, and that was the wonder of it, that what was private and unspeakable before is speakable now because you speak it"* (162).

The Tetzlar telescope also functions to locate Kitty Vaught for Will. Searching for the peregrine falcon in Central Park, Will finds instead a beautiful young girl and falls in love with her at a distance of 2,000 feet. It is not just Kitty's good looks that attract Will. Like Binx Bolling, Will thinks he sees himself in Kitty; he identifies her as the other with whom he can live a life:

> It was not so much her good looks, her smooth brushed brow and firm round neck bowed so that two or three vertebrae surfaced in the soft flesh, as a certain bemused and dry-eyed expression in which he seemed to recognize—himself! . . . She was his better half. It would be possible to sit on a bench and eat a peanut-butter sandwich with her and not say a word (8).

Because Kitty reminds him of himself, Will sees the possibility of sharing the simplest of lives with her, enjoying the world together. Later in South Carolina, he tells Kitty: "I had wanted to be with you during the ordinary times of the day, for example after breakfast in the morning" (165).

Although Will tends to think in outmoded romantic imagery of what life would be like with Kitty—he dreams of "holding her charms in his arms" and of living with her "in a cottage small by the waterfall" (166)—he actually wants to share everything with her, and thus to know her. In New York, Kitty appears to be cut adrift and in need of Will, her ambition of defining herself as a dancer having come to nothing despite the fact that she has devoted ten years to studying ballet (114). Yet, despite their mutual needs, Will and Kitty do not manage to establish an intersubjective relationship. They are always "out of phase," as Will describes it. If one of them is open to talking and getting through to the other, something is wrong with the other. When Kitty and Will do communicate, there is no depth to their conversations. Their failure to meet on an ontological level is attested to by their failure on a sexual level.[13]

Two important scenes illustrate their failure to find each other. Will first attempts to make love to Kitty in Central Park in what he names "the sniper's den" because it reminds him of a Civil War photograph taken by Matthew Brady. The name is not auspicious, and the lovemaking is not completed. Will knows that he needs Kitty, but he is not sure that this need means that he loves her: "Love, he thought, and all at once the word itself went opaque and curious, a little howling business behind the front teeth. Do I love her? I something her" (104). When Kitty strips and comes into his arms, Will is astonished by the reality of her flesh, "the terrific immediacy of it" (108), but Kitty is not available to Will because her sexual overture amounts to only "a little experiment by Kitty for the benefit of Kitty," to prove to herself that she is a normal girl, that she can make love like anyone else (109). The circumstances are further complicated by the fact that Kitty is slightly drugged with hikuli tea and therefore is beyond herself, not really present in the park with Will. She herself has gone away, removed to some scientific level where she can observe and evaluate her own performance as lover.

Like Binx and Kate on the train to Chicago, Will and Kitty are unable to consummate their love sexually because they are both too abstracted from their bodies to inhabit them:

> Yet when at last the hard-pressed but courteous and puisant engineer did see the way clear to sustaining the two of them, her in passing her test, him lest he be demoralized by Perlmutter's heaven, too much heaven too soon, and fail them both—well, I do love her, he saw clearly, and therefore I shall—it was too late (110).

Just as he is beginning to feel that he might be able to bring it off, Kitty becomes sick and Will notes the truth of their relationship: "Even their sicknesses alternated and were out of phase" (111).

Another important encounter between Will and Kitty occurs at Folly Beach, South Carolina. But just as suggested in the Sniper's

Den episode, the name of the place prefigures an ominous fate. Although Folly Beach in the moonlight provides an ideal environment for lovers, Will and Kitty are drawn farther apart than ever. Appropriate to the romantic setting, each declares love for the other, but the language does not convince, the words "I love you" do not coincide with their meaning, and thus Will wonders, "Why did this not sound right, here on Folly Beach in old Carolina in the moonlight?" (166). Again their lovemaking fails, a debacle telegraphed by their awkward manuevering to position their bodies:

> When he leaned over again and embraced her in the sand, he knowing without calculating the exact angle at which he might lie over against her—about twenty degrees past the vertical—she miscalculated, misread him and moved slightly, yet unmistakably to get plainly and simply under him, then feeling the surprise in him stopped almost before she began. It was like correcting a misstep in dancing (166–67).

Kitty's physical clumsiness amounts to a metaphor for her ontological dis-ease. She is still trying to prove herself sexually, while Will is determined to court her in the proper way, "no more grubby epithalial embraces in dogbane thickets" (166). Therefore, they are utterly out of rhythm with one another, no "I" and "thou" coming together in a harmonious intersubjective relationship.

Evidently blind to his own dogged performance, Will can see through Kitty's impersonation, that she has adopted a role essentially for the benefit of a third person (herself and/or another):

> But what threw him off worst was that, sentient as always, he found himself catching onto how it was with her: he saw that she was out to be a proper girl and taking every care to do the right wrong thing. There were even echoes of a third person: what, you worry about the boys as good a figure as you have, etc. So he was the boy and she was doing her best to do what a girl does (167).

Will is, of course, correct. In Marcel's terms, Kitty is the *poseur*, taking the part of a woman making love instead of inhabiting her own body and fully giving herself: "to pose is always to pose before oneself. 'To play to the gallery,' we are accustomed to say, but the gallery is still the self. . . . we might say that the other person is the provisional and as it were necessary medium through which I can arrive at forming a certain image, or idol of myself" (*HV* 18). Sensing that Kitty is not wholly present with him, Will becomes more and more unhappy. Yet he is sufficiently concerned about Kitty's self-image that he offers her the very impersonation she needs: "Very well, I'll be both for you, boyfriend and girlfriend, lover and father. If it is possible." And he even manages to kiss her "somewhat lewdly" so that Kitty won't feel that she has failed in her role of seductress (167).

Once she returns to her home in the South, Kitty begins to act out other roles: the perfect little coed, a sorority girl, a football fan. These roles fulfill the hopes she has expressed to Sutter's ex-wife Rita in New York:

> I want to go to dances and get a tremendous rush. That's what my grandmother used to say: I went to such and such a dance and got a tremendous rush. . . . I want to go to school. I want to buy new textbooks and a binder full of fresh paper and hold my books in my arms and walk across the campus. And wear a sweater. . . . I want to go to the Sugar Bowl (171).

Kitty gets her wish to be a coed, wearing the obligatory cashmere sweater; she becomes a football fan and a cheerleader; and, in short, she becomes Percy's ideal consumer, consuming the college experience after the idealized fashion of her grandmother's old tales. And she seems happy.[14] Completely "at home" at the university, Kitty has sunk into the dangerous despair "that does not know itself" as despair.[15] To the extent that these impersonations satisfy her, Kitty cannot be available to Will as the needy "other." She therefore jeopardizes her identity in the way that Marcel argues the *poseur* inevitably does: "From that moment that I become preoccupied about the effect I want to produce on the other person, my every act, word and attitude loses its authenticity" (*HV* 17).

Once Kitty becomes comfortable with her role as college coed, she develops mannerisms. Instead of allowing her eyes to meet Will's in a look that could establish intersubjectivity, Kitty shies away from real intimacy, preferring to consume the packaged intimacy at the university: "Since she had become a coed, Kitty had given up her actress's lilt for a little trite sorority cry which was made with her eyes going away" (228).

Where we can most clearly see the contrast between Will and Kitty is in their differing responses to the university where they enroll. Will, who usually feels bad in "good" environments, recoils from the fallacious good cheer at the university, which Percy ironically expresses: "Naturally in such an intersubjective paradise as this, he soon got the proper horrors" (204). Kitty, on the other hand, fits in well at the university, so well that its doings become more important to her than the wishes of her dying brother or her love for Will. Although Jamie longs to go west and Will wants to accompany him, Kitty does not want to leave because she doesn't want to miss the Big Game between her school and Tennessee.

When the intersubjective relationship between Will and Kitty is blocked by Kitty's consumer self, Sutter Vaught moves to the foreground of the novel to become the other for whom Will searches. Significantly, just after Will names Kitty's impersonation for the first time, Sutter appears. As Will sleeps under a crape myrtle in the Vaught garden, Kitty slips up and kisses him. Will dreams that a young woman has stooped to kiss him and says to her: "Very well, little Hebe. Be Betty coed and have your little fun on Flirtation Walk. . . . Drain your cup, little Hebe, then let me know when you want to get down to business" (205).[16] Although this short scene receives no particular emphasis, it is important because here Will names Kitty for what she has become, a flirtatious girl who is playing games with him, no longer the lost person with whom he thought he could make a life:

> But it was his own Kitty who had been most mysteriously transformed. . . . No longer was she the solitary girl on the park bench, as inward and watchful as he, who might wander with him through old Louisiana, perch on the back step of the camper of an evening with the same shared sense of singularity of time and the excellence of place. No, she was Miss Katherine Gibbs Vaught and the next thing he knew she'd have her picture in the *Commercial Appeal* (260–61).[17]

We are prepared for Sutter's eventual importance in the novel when Will Barrett first meets the Vaught family in the hospital in New York where Jamie is undergoing chemotherapy. In the hospital, Will is confronted by Chandler Vaught, the father who assumes that Will is a doctor and who asks him, "Do you know Sutter, my oldest boy? He's a doctor like you" (53). From the first mention of his name, then, we have introduced the possible similarity of Will and Sutter. Will is so suggestible that Mr. Vaught's calling attention to someone who is *like* him is enough to interest him in who Sutter might be. Shortly thereafter, Rita is introduced to Will as the woman who "married my oldest boy, Sutter Vaught. Dr. Vaught" (58). Notably, Sutter's credentials are stressed: he is a doctor; he is a scientist who has published in learned journals and is therefore an expert; he reads books by Wittgenstein—all this during Will's first encounter with the Vaught family. The fact that Will hears Sutter's name even before he learns Kitty's (the "news" that Will thinks he most needs) is no doubt Percy's strategic way of anticipating Sutter's significance. For as Percy has admitted, "Sutter is a very pivotal character in the book—he is the object of Barrett's quest, and he must seem very substantial."[18]

When Sutter enters the novel in the flesh, he appears as an evocation of Milton's Satan, an ominous presence who stands looking over the garden at Will and Kitty: "Some thirty feet away and ten feet above him [on] a balcony . . . there stood a man . . . with his hands in his pockets, looking down into the garden" (206). Even in his confusion, Will takes note of this oldest of the Vaught offspring. He perceives Sutter as "both merry and haggard," a man whose most notable quality is his thinness. When Sutter turns his head, Will observes: "There was something wrong with his cheek, a shadowing, a distinguished complication like a German saber scar" (207). Rather than a war wound, however, the scar turns out to be the detritus of a suicide attempt, which Sutter has described in his casebook: "Went to ranch, shot myself, missed brain, carried away cheek" (373).

While staying with the Vaught family in Atlanta, Will has only four private conversations with Sutter, the last two the night before Sutter and Jamie leave for Santa Fe. Having been prepared to accept Sutter as an expert diagnostician by Kitty's comment, "Sutter could look at you and tell what was wrong with you" (114), Will tries to get Sutter to tell him what has caused his amnesia. He also wants to know if Sutter thinks that his "nervous condition" might be the result of not having sexual intercourse. But Sutter refuses to enlighten Will because he understands that Will's "posture is self-defeating," that Will's search for the right expert to give him direction is preventing him from living his own life (353). Even as he tells Will that he is no savant, Sutter establishes a connection with him: "Who do you think I am, for Christ's sake: I am no guru and I want no disciples. You've come to the wrong man. Or did you expect that?" Sutter looked at him keenly (225). Unlike Kitty, who cannot look at Will without her "eyes going away" (205, 228, 247), Sutter does commune with Will through eye contact.

Consequently, we are prepared for the development of an inter-subjective relationship between these two men, which seems to develop during their fourth meeting. This guarantees that Will will follow Sutter and that his strongest tie from this point on in the novel will be to him. In this meeting, Will seeks Sutter's help because he cannot sleep. After planting a posthypnotic suggestion allowing Will to sleep, Sutter suggests that the next few days should bring developments making it possible for Will to act. And then Sutter concludes with a curious offer: "If you find yourself in too tight a spot, that is, in a situation where it is difficult to live from one minute to the next, come and see me and I'll help you. I may not be here, but you can find me" (271). The rest of the novel focuses on Will's accepting this invitation,[19] as he follows a route west marked on Sutter's road map, and as he decides at some primitive level of consciousness that Sutter is a more compelling other than Kitty:

> No wonder he was confused. He had forgotten Kitty and left her at the university and now remembered nothing more than that he had forgotten. There was only the nameless tug pulling him back. But he had also forgotten what Sutter told him the night before—*come find me*—and recorded only the huge tug forward in the opposite direction. He shrugged: well, I'm not going back because I've been there (294).

By following Sutter even when he is unconscious of the pursuit, Will implicitly grants what Marcel says about the connection between trust and the presence of a "thou":

> To believe in someone, is to put one's trust in him, i.e.: 'I am sure you will not let me down, that you will instead fulfill my expecta-

tions, that you will realize them.' I expressly use the second person here. One can only trust a 'thou', a reality capable of fulfilling the function of a 'thou', of being invoked, of becoming something I can fall back on (*CF* 135).

For a while, Will's only clue to Sutter's identity appears in Sutter's casebook, a journal as deeply preoccupied with death as Will is. The casebook begins with notes for an autopsy, written in the shorthand of a man familiar with the procedure: "A w.d. and n. white male, circa 49" (279). These are the notes for a formal report that begins, "This is the body of a well-developed and nourished white male, about forty-nine." Here, Sutter explores his theory that, through the veneration of science, humans have become so removed from the world of ordinary human experience (the immanent) that they have difficulty returning from their transcendent orbit. In order for the abstracted human to be assured that the self is real, the individual engages in sexual intercourse, which only causes more loneliness than ever. Proof of Sutter's theory is contained in his exploration of "The Incidence of Post-orgasmic Suicide in Male University Graduate Students" (65).

Although it starts out as a coroner's casebook, the notebook, composed of disconnected fragments, rapidly becomes a record of Sutter's own deteriorating condition, his progress toward death. Part of the journal is also a dialogue carried on with his sister Val, a Roman Catholic nun:

> I do not deny, Val, that a revival of your sacramental system is an alternative to lewdness (the only other alternative is the forgetting of the old sacrament), for lewdness itself is a kind of sacrament (devilish, if you like). The difference is that my sacrament is operational and yours is not (281).

Since Sutter is withdrawn from his fellow beings, it is appropriate that, rather than confronting Val directly in the intersubjective experience of dialogue, he controls the imaginary debate with Val. If he were open to Val, he would be willing to take the risk of allowing her to argue with him, to reveal herself to him, to be a person and not just a representative of the Church he has rejected.

When Will catches up with Sutter in Santa Fe, he tells Sutter that he has been reading the casebook. Sutter's response is telling: "It is of no importance. Everything in it is either wrong or irrelevant. Throw it away" (360). Sutter's dismissal of what he has written reminds us of Marcel's admonition that a person's opinions do not tell us who he is: "Nothing is less able to illuminate a being for us, less able to show his worth or what he is than knowing what his opinions are; opinions do not count" (*CF* 78). Despite Sutter's instructions, Will finishes the journal before throwing it away. Lying in the Trav-L-Aire, Will reads the last entry, which provides significant news of Sutter's condition:

> Went to ranch, shot myself, missed brain, carried away cheek. Recovery in hospital. . . . I saw something clearly while I had no cheek and grinned like a skeleton. But I got well and forgot what it was. I won't miss next time (373).

This last entry suggests that Sutter has abandoned his journal because, having decided to kill himself, he no longer needs to record his thoughts or to justify his decision. Sutter may also leave it behind, as Lewis Lawson suggests, so that Will Barrett will read it and see that Sutter is a failure, a desperately unhappy man with no idea of how to live in the world.[20] There is the additional implication that by leaving his notebook with the road map where Will can find it, Sutter is making a faint cry for help, reaching out for the other, Will Barrett, who may be able to decipher the message in the last entry. Later, Sutter tells Will that he does not intend to live after Jamie dies. Responding to Sutter's request that he make the arrangements for getting the family to Santa Fe, Will asks Sutter where he will be and Sutter replies, "If I do outlive Jamie . . . it will not be by more than two hours. What in Christ's name do you think I'm doing out here: Do you think I'm staying? Do you think I'm going back?" (389). Sutter's blatant declaration of his suicidal plans causes, for the first time, a shock of recognition in Will: "Perhaps this moment more than any other, the moment of his first astonishment, marked the beginning for the engineer of what is called a normal life" (389).

Sutter's death wish, his obsession with "the certain availability of death," connects him to Will Barrett's father, Lawyer Ed Barrett, and thus, more inevitably than ever, to Will (373). Marcel's comments on suicide pertain to both men: "The thought of our own death, of the only future event we can acknowledge as certain, can exercise a fascination over us in a way that somehow invades our whole field of experience, extinguishing all our joys" (*CF* 173). Sutter Vaught and Ed Barrett are alike in several ways. Both have been failed by the systems they expected would sustain them, the failure of romanticism and stoicism in Lawyer Barrett's case, the failure of science in Sutter's. Both men live without hope and are therefore Marcel's potential suicides. In *Being and Having*, Marcel says: "The soul lives by hope alone; hope is perhaps the very stuff of which our souls are made. . . . To despair of one's self—is it not anticipating suicide? (*BH* 80).

In addition, both men have problems with transcendence and with returning to the immanent world. Cut off from the immanent world of others, neither Will's father nor Sutter can find a way to live, which leads to their turning to suicide as a last resort. On a symbolic level, the part of the body at which each man aims the weapon betrays the failure of their systems. Will's father, whose romanticism has proved nugatory, aims at his heart, "fitting the muzzle into the notch of his breastbone" (331); and Sutter, whose scientific objectivity has also proved inconsequential, aims at the center of intellectual pursuit, the brain.

The ultimate importance of Sutter's suicidal effort is that it forces Will to confront his father's death, to break through repeated memories of his father's nocturnal walks under the water oaks in front of his house and focus on the evening that Ed Barrett took his own life. It was on the same evening that he had won a great victory over the people in town against whom he had been fighting, for these enemies had suddenly pulled out. But having no hope for the future of humanity, Ed Barrett considers his victory as merely Pyrrhic. It means nothing to him because, as he tells his son, "They"—the "fornicators and the bribers and the takers of bribes" —have won after all (330). There are no longer any noble people of principle; there are no longer any distinctions between fornicators and gentlemen. Lawyer Barrett suffers from the world-weariness reflected in his favorite poem, "Dover Beach," (309) and in Brahms's Great Horn Theme, "the very sound of the ruined gorgeousness of the nineteenth century, the worst of times," to which he listens as he strolls back and forth in front of his house on De Ridder (100). In his romantic cynicism, Lawyer Barrett retreats from the world into a nostalgic yearning for the bygone days when a gentleman could face down the leader of the Ku Klux Klan in the street.

Will's father has nothing to replace the system which has failed him; and he offers no indication that he has any sense of intersubjectivity or that he loves his son, who desperately needs him. His suicide provides the worst kind of abandonment, what Marcel calls "an absolute desertion," because he leaves his son without a father (*BH* 142). In *Creative Fidelity*, Marcel notes that suicide is "the temptation-type, the betrayal type, and all other temptations and betrayals can perhaps be reduced to it" (*CF* 173). Moreover, Marcel's harsh judgment of the stoic also applies to Ed Barrett: "The stoic is always imprisoned within himself. He strengthens himself, no doubt, but he does not radiate. . . . He bears himself— and that means that above all he controls his interior life—as though he had no neighbors, as though he were concerned only with himself and had no responsibility towards anyone else" (*HV* 38). Hence, Ed Barrett tells young Will, "In the last analysis, you are alone" (331). Since he is unavailable to himself and to others, he thinks that he can dispose of himself by "falling on his sword" as any good Roman who saw no alternative but defeat would do. In Marcel's terms, Ed Barrett's suicide is the last resort of a man who is already completely non-available to others; by the act, he renders himself forever after unavailable (*BH* 124).

Because Will has lived with one despairing man whose abstraction from life led him to suicide, when he leaves the South to follow Sutter and Jamie to Santa Fe, he takes a step that leads ultimately to the possibility of his redeeming the past by saving the despairing Sutter Vaught. After an experience in front of his old home on De Ridder Street during which he finally remembers his father's suicide, Will has a reverse Sartrean experience with the *en-soi*, the objects of the world. As Will moves his fingers over the iron horsehead on the hitching post in front of his father's house, he has an encounter with reality that provides an alternative to his father's despair. Of his father's search, Will concludes:

> He had missed it! It was not in the Brahms that one looked and not
> in solitariness and not in the old sad poetry but—he wrung out his
> ear—but here, under your nose, here in the very curiousness and

drollness and extraness of the iron and the bark that—he shook his head—that— (332).

The sentence breaks off, but Will seems to have experienced an intimation of the comfort to be found in the very solid existence of objects. There is the possibility that a life lived with other people among named objects could be an alternative to his father's solitariness, his rejection of others. Will seems to find comfort in the physical world of objects.[21]

Having finally remembered his father's suicide, Will is freed from the past by his own acknowledgement that his father was wrong to choose death. Shortly after Will arrives in Santa Fe, Jamie becomes very ill. Finally, acting on Val's orders, Will summons a priest to baptize Jamie. Although his spiritual sensitivity allows him to serve as a vehicle of grace, an interpreter for Father Boomer of Jamie's muddled responses, Will has little if any conscious idea of what happens during the baptism. For such cognition, he needs Sutter; but Sutter declines any explanation beyond "You were there" (407). Yet their bearing witness to Jamie's death, which includes the evacuation of Jamie's bowels—"the dread ultimate rot of the molecules themselves"—does inextricably unite Will and Sutter (401). Rationally conceived or not, what they share is in keeping with Marcel's suggestion that an "ordeal endured in common" is often prefatory to the establishment of intersubjectivity, especially if the event is "a really incommunicable experience— generally a painful one—about which the initiated feel that others, who did not share it in the flesh, have no right to speak" (MB 1: 222–23). This shared secret, like the one Binx and Kate have of feeling the guilt of the survivor, binds Will and Sutter together.

Notwithstanding his failure to grasp the significance of the baptism (the moment of grace that allows Jamie to respond to Father Boomer), Will achieves a *concrete* realization of the *abstraction* of death in the horrible individual death of Jamie Vaught. The influence of this realization can be seen later, when Will runs after Sutter on the street in Santa Fe, for he speaks on an individual, concrete level. As Sutter tries to leave Will behind in order to go to his ranch, probably with the intention of committing suicide, Will calls after him four times, "Wait," even taking hold of Sutter's sleeve to restrain him (408). Finally Will says the right thing, supplying the missing word to the incomplete sentence that he first addressed to his father: "Dr. Vaught, don't leave me" (409). Not just, "don't leave," but "don't leave *me*." At last Will makes the real request of a man who does not want to be left alone. But Sutter initially fails to understand this personal note, thinking that in trying to prevent his suicide Will has in mind only lost contributions to humanity. Thus Will must offer an even further, more straightforward declaration of his own need:

> "Dr. Vaught, I need you. I, Will Barrett—" and he actually pointed to himself lest there be a mistake, "—need you and want you to come back. I need you more than Jamie needed you. Jamie had Val too" (409).

The very specific concrete language which Will uses here is the opposite of the empty abstract language he used when he suggested to Sutter that it is best "to cultivate whatever talents one has," and "to make a contribution, however small" (384, 385). Stated in these terms, the ideas have no bearing on an individual, and Sutter has no reason to respond because he has heard such meaningless platitudes many times.[22]

By naming himself and specifying his need, Will engages in a gesture suggesting a symbolic baptism, one in which he not only positions himself as a potential recipient but also offers himself as a gift. Through the simple declarations of "I need" and "I want," Will makes his appeal as a gift quite clear, suggesting Marcel's idea that "Each one of us is in a position to recognize that his own essence is a gift . . . that he himself is a gift" (*MB* 1: 194). And confronted by such a personal gift, Sutter must, according to Marcel, respond (*HV* 62). Whereas Sutter has no response to Will's general call that he make a contribution to humanity, he now has in front of him one achingly real individual, a subject who encounters him as a "thou." Will's gesture therefore contains what might prove to be a moment of grace for Sutter. That would seem to be the tentative conclusion, when, in response to Will's fifth "Wait," Sutter stops the Edsel and waits for Will to catch up. The novel ends inconclusively but with a note of hope. Finally someone waits for Will Barrett, who has spent the whole novel trying to catch up.

Tom More's Lapsometer

A High Tech Alternative to Intersubjectivity

Percy's third novel, *Love in the Ruins*, is a rollicking satire that is also a comedy in Dante's Christian sense. The novel ends with an ultimately hopeful message of reconciliation and brotherhood for its protagonist, Dr. Tom More, who, in the course of the present action, discovers that love is indeed possible even in the ruins of a 45-year-old life.

Before Tom More reaches his happy ending, however, he lives as a despairing and damned man, devoting his time to drinking gin fizzes, lusting after women, and working on his invention, the lapsometer, with which he expects both to cure the ills that beset the spirit of humankind and to win the Nobel Prize. Much of the novel is concerned with the lapsometer as a tool which offers an alternative to intersubjectivity as the solution to the individual's problems with self and others. Tom More—self-proclaimed genius, confident of his ability to solve the problem of the fallen nature of humankind, drunk as a lord during much of the novel, filled with pride, determined to have all three of the "girls" he has stowed away in the Howard Johnson's motel—believes that his invention, More's Qualitative-Quantitative Ontological Lapsometer (MOQUOL), can measure the degree to which a person's soul fails to coincide with itself and thus save modern humankind from itself. He employs an empirical approach to what he chooses to think of as the "problem" of being. Once the shabby modern incarnation of the devil, Art Immelmann, shows More how to add an ionizer to the lapsometer, More is able to "treat" as well as diagnose. After the ionizer is added to the lapsometer, however, all hell breaks loose, demonstrating Marcel's contention that modern humankind is increasingly less able to control its own technological inventions.[1] Ultimately science fails Tom More just as it did Sutter Vaught. Only when the lapsometer falls into Immelmann's very wrong hands, and when More is confronted with losing his nurse Ellen Oglethorpe to Immelmann, does he manage a spontaneous prayer that miraculously saves him.

In *Love in the Ruins*, more than in any of his other novels, Percy presents Marcel's "broken world," about which Marcel wrote a play, *Le Monde cassé*, and to which he devoted an entire chapter in *The Mystery of Being*. Because he sees the world as broken, Marcel stresses the importance of incarnation, participation, and ultimately intersubjectivity in order to restore ontological weight to Being. Describing the world that he saw in 1950, Marcel wrote:

> This is one preliminary point that must occur to all of us; we live today in a world at war with itself, and this state of world-war is being pushed so far that it runs the risk of ending in something that could properly be described as world-suicide. . . . Suicide, until our own times, was an individual possibility. . . . It seems now to apply to the case of the whole human world (*MB* 1: 28).

The world of *Love in the Ruins* is also broken: "The center did not hold," Tom More says, borrowing from Yeats and proceeding to describe political polarization between the Knotheads (the old Republican party) and the Leftpapas (the old Democrats).[2] The Catholic Church has broken into schisms, with only a small remnant remaining faithful to the Pope in Rome. An unpopular war that has further divided the country has been raging in Ecuador for 15 years.

Against this backdrop of divisions, More narrows the focus of his narration to a region somewhere near New Orleans, made up of the unnamed town where he practices medicine; a government complex, "Fedville," which includes Love Clinic, the Geriatric Rehabilitation facility, and a hospital where More is on "patient-staff status" (203); Paradise Estates, a suburban development where More lives, "an oasis of concord in a troubled land" (17) where "Knothead lives next to Leftist in peace" (19); and Honey Island swamp where live "the dropouts and castoffs of and rebels against our society" (15), primarily Bantus and Hippies.[3] Although the novel, published in 1971, is set in 1983, its concerns and the people who inhabit it make it very much a novel of the sixties. At night More obsessively reads Stedmann's *History of World War I*, in which he finds Marcel's suicidal modern world detailed: "For weeks now I've been on the Battle of Verdun, which killed half a million men, lasted a year, and left the battle lines unchanged. Here began the hemorrhage and death by suicide of the old Western World" (47).

So much does More emphasize the divisions that have occurred between left and right, young and old, black and white, that we are likely to miss at first the important evidence that he himself is a broken man. In the first section of the novel, dated July 4, we discover that More is an alcoholic whose eyes are swelling closed because he is allergic to the gin fizzes he has been drinking. Only gradually do we discover that he has been living in despair since his daughter Samantha's death seven years ago from a neuroblastoma which "pushed one eye out and around the nosebridge so that Samantha looked like a two-eyed Picasso profile" (72). Throughout the novel, More remembers the times he spent with Samantha in that golden summer of his life before she died:

> The best of times were after mass on summer evenings when Samantha and I would walk home in the violet dusk, we having received Communion and I rejoicing afterwards, caring nought for my fellow Catholics but only for myself and Samantha and Christ swallowed, remembering what he promised me for eating him, that I would have life in me, and I did, feeling so good that I'd sing and cut the fool all the way home like King David before the Ark (12–13).

After Samantha's death, both More and his wife Doris blamed God for their loss. Doris ran away with a "heathen Englishman" (11, 20, 24, 64) who offered her spiritual comfort. More lost his hold on his own life and the intersubjective relationship he had had with his daughter, and retaliated against the God in whom he still believes by neglecting to go to Mass. He began drinking heavily and turned away from the intersubjective world of the Church, redoubling his efforts in science, partly to take his mind off his loss, partly because he had had earlier successes in the field.

And so More finally comes to believe that he has invented a machine that will locate problems which are deeply embedded in human nature by reading the various Brodmann sections of the brain. With his invention, More scans the brain and makes Marcel's discovery about the self:

> If you measure the pineal activity of a monkey—or any subhuman animal—with my lapsometer, you will invariably record identical readings at Layers I and II. Its self, that is to say, coincides with itself. Only in man do you find a discrepancy; Layer I, the outer social self, ticking over, say, at a sprightly 5.4 mmv, while Layer II just lies there, barely alive at 0.7 mmv, or even zero!—a nought, a gap, an aching wound. Only in man does the self miss itself, *fall* from itself (hence lapsometer) [36].

What More here describes in terms of Levels I and II is exactly what Marcel designates as the contradiction that all human beings face when they try to find themselves by asking themselves who they are. The human "self" that does not coincide with itself is, in Marcel's terms, as in More's, a wound:

> Burdened with myself, plunged in this disturbing world . . . I keep an eager lookout for everything emanating from it which might either soothe or ulcerate the wound I bear within me, which is my *ego*. What then is this anguish, this wound? The answer is that it is above all the experience of being torn by a contradiction between the all which I aspire to possess, to annex, or, still more absurd, to monopolize, and the obscure consciousness that after all I am nothing but an empty void (*HV* 16).[4]

Marcel's solution to the problem of the aching wound of the ego is that each person must seek out others: "Hence this craving to be confirmed from outside, by another; this paradox, by virtue of which even the most self-centered among us looks to others and only to others for his final investiture" (*HV* 16).

Dr. More, however, not content with philosophical solutions to spiritual questions, hopes to perfect the lapsometer so that he will be able to treat as well as diagnose the aching wound of self: "Suppose I could hit on the right dosage and weld the broken self whole! What if man could reenter paradise, so to speak, and live there both as man and spirit, whole and intact man-spirit, as solid flesh as a speckled trout, a dappled thing, yet aware of itself as a self!" (36). The very name of the device, "More's Qualitative-Quantitative Ontological Lapsometer," shows the enormous undertaking that More plans for himself. Dr. More believes that he can be both physician and metaphysician, ignoring Marcel's clear distinction between the metaproblematic world of the metaphysician and the problematic world of the scientist. Early in his career Marcel noted, "It is important to show at the outset that metaphysics always claims to be the satisfaction of uneasiness, whereas scientific knowledge is quite different and there is no such thing as scientific uneasiness" (*MJ* 293). The individual's sense of dis–ease and metaphysical uneasiness cannot be treated with the objective-empirical methods of science.

Furthermore, when Tom More uses the adjective "ontological" to describe the lapsometer, he takes on a study that greater minds than his have grappled with. Ontology has as its subject no simpler a question than "What is the nature of Being?" Both Heidegger and Marcel saw early on that the question of being has a logically anterior question which must first be considered: What is the nature of the being who calls Being into question? Heidegger saw Dasein (human being) as the being among all others who could ask questions about Being. Marcel argued that the question "What is Being?" has as a prior question, "Who am I who can ask what is being?"[5]

More plans to use his lapsometer to focus on the individual being of the subject under consideration, assuming that empirical science can solve problems and answer such philosophical questions. He thus ignores Marcel's admonition that Being cannot be approached as if it were a problem that is separate from the investigator:

> We become more and more convinced that, strictly speaking, there is no problem of Being and no problematic approach to it. . . . we have acquired the execrable habit of considering the problems in themselves, that is, in abstraction from the manner in which their appearance is woven into the very texture of life. A scientist is privileged in this respect. A scientific problem arises at a given point in his research, it is something the mind stumbles upon as the foot stumbles upon a stone (*BH* 102).

To try to understand Being by using problematic (empirical)

approaches is to ignore that "knowledge is within being, enfolded by it" (*BH* 115). The *problem* of Being is therefore really the *mystery* of Being because the questioner cannot subtract himself from Being in order to study it. In like manner, the relationship between soul and body is also more than a problem; it is a mystery which can be addressed only by recognizing an individual's ontological status as incarnated being (*BH* 111).[6] Marcel argues that the metaphysician can only approach Being phenomenologically by focusing on those spiritual aspects of being which are uniquely human. He directs the investigator toward considerations of· "fidelity, hope, and love where we may see man at grips with the temptations of denial, introversion, and hard-heartedness" (*BH* 119). More, however, believes that his lapsometer "gives promise of bridging the dread chasm between body and mind that has sundered the soul of Western man for five hundred years" (90). All his experimentation with the lapsometer is doomed to failure, though, because he approaches human nature as a problem to be solved rather than as a mystery in which he is himself involved. Tom claims to be a metaphysician, but in developing the lapsometer he employs a device that will *condition* the individual out of problems with self, just as the behaviorists he condemns condition human beings in the Skinner box.

More's colleagues, although they are lampooned for their behaviorist methods in the Love Clinic and their support of euthanasia, at least have the good sense to reject discussions of metaphysics. They seem to realize that empirical knowledge has its limits and that it is not the business of science to deal with metaphysics. Colley Wilkes, for example, who helped More make his first working model of the lapsometer, is interested in the lapsometer only as a tool to locate brain tumors, an appropriate pursuit for the doctor. Even More's good friend, Max Gottlieb, expresses his skepticism. Commenting on More's scholarly paper on the lapsometer, Max says, "I think you've hit on something extremely intriguing. You've got a gift for correlation, but there's too much subjectivity here and your series is too short" (114). Max reminds More that a scientific theory must rest on solid experimental evidence. Max Gottlieb also warns Tom that his lapsometer falls outside the purview of science: "Well now. The soul of Western man, that's a large order, Tom. Besides being rather uh metaphysical—" (115).

What is very much absent from Tom More's ontological pursuits with the lapsometer is the sense of wonder that the consideration of Being always evokes in philosophers. Heidegger, for example, after he had conducted a phenomenological examination of Nothing, saw as the basic question of metaphysics: "Why are there beings at all, and why not rather nothing?"[7] Heidegger's question reveals his astonishment. Given the possibility of Nothingness, he expresses wonder and reverence at the realization of all the entities in Dasein's world. Marcel also stresses the wonder of the philosopher who confronts the ontological mystery: "Whoever philosophizes *hic et nunc*, is, it may be said, a prey of reality; he will never become completely accustomed to the fact of existing; existence is inseparable from a certain astonishment" (*CF* 63–64).

Enraptured by the lapsometer, Tom More lacks the metaphysician's awe when confronted by the mystery of Being. As Lewis Lawson and J. Gerald Kennedy point out, More, who claims to have created the device that will weld the self whole again after Descartes has torn it apart, is himself a thoroughgoing Cartesian. Lawson observes that More even locates the soul where Descartes located it, in the pineal gland.[8] When More assumes that he can render the broken self whole and return human beings to their prelapsarian state, he is in great danger of sinning against Being. If everything can be explained away—including the person's very nature, individual creatureliness and soul—then we can no longer see anything at which to marvel, and the Creation disappears into a void made by our own attempts to explain it.

The broken selves of individuals exist within the broken world Marcel has described, which he attributes to the spirit of abstraction that is loose in the twentieth century as a result of our increasing belief in empiricism, science and totalitarian systems to tell us who we are. Commenting on Marxism's inability to deal with metaphysical uneasiness, Marcel imagines with foreboding a time when "metaphysical uneasiness would be considered as a psychosomatic malady and would be treated according to the appropriate medical rules" (*MB* 1: 43). Tom More's lapsometer, which would make it possible to treat metaphysical uneasiness by "appropriate medical rules" once Art Immelmann adds the ionizer and announces a plan that will put a MOQUOL "in the hands of every physician and social scientist in the U.S. within one year's time," seems to be the fulfillment of Marcel's worst dreams (169).

Tom More, who sees exactly the same broken world that absorbed Marcel, decides that he can heal the fissure in the human being with a device made possible by the empirical means that Marcel rules out. Agreeing with Marcel that the modern individual is dominated by the spirit of abstraction, More names the condition "angelism," a term he borrows from Jacques Maritain.[9] Angelism, defined by More as "excessive abstraction of the self from itself" (37), is Sutter Vaught's transcendence under another name. Angelism occurs when a person spends a great deal of time among abstractions because it is difficult, as Sutter points out, for the scientist to re-enter the immanent world. In order to assure themselves that they are real, abstracted persons engage in sex to remind themselves that they are incarnated creatures and not pure mind. At the opposite pole from angelism in Tom More's system is "bestialism," or "adjustment to the environment" (27). Here, the person is little more than an organism in an environment, concerned solely with satisfying the needs of the body. Dr. More explains that the two conditions are not mutually exclusive: "It is not uncommon nowadays to see patients suffering from angelism-bestialism. A man, for example, can feel at one and the same time extremely abstracted and inordinately lustful toward lovely young women who may be perfect strangers" (27).

More himself exhibits both tendencies. In his desire to perfect his lapsometer and win the Nobel Prize, he is all angelism; in his pursuit of Lola Rhoades and Moira Schaffner, he is all bestialism. More admits that he is the chief example in his study: "It is my misfortune—and blessing—that I suffer from both liberal and conservative complaints, e.g., both morning terror and large-bowel disorders, excessive abstraction and unseasonable rages, alternating impotence and satyriasis. So that at one and the same time I have great sympathy for my patients and lead a fairly miserable life" (20).

As always in Percy's novels, ordeal can be the occasion of the protagonist's coming to himself. In this case, the ordeal that provides the beginning of More's possible redemption is his attempted suicide on Christmas Eve, six months before the present action of the novel. In a number a flashback sequences, More remembers that Christmas Eve in particularly sharp detail because on that day he finished his lapsometer article for *Brain*. Lonely in his success, he drinks gin fizzes with Lola Rhoades and tells her about his lapsometer. Later, they make love in a bunker on the golf course just before Tom passes out from an allergic reaction to albumen.

At home alone on Christmas Eve, Tom watches the Perry Como Christmas show. He suffers from terrible despair, the result of coming down from the high of finishing his article combined with post-coital sadness. He does not remember cutting his wrists. Instead he remembers coming to himself to discover his wrists bleeding and wanting to live: "I came to myself, saw myself as itself and the world for what it is, and began to love life" (97). It apparently takes the wound to the body to restore More to a sense of his incarnated being, to remind him that he *has* a body, and to return him from his abstract orbit to the immanent world. Just as Binx Bolling comes to himself one morning and sees the objects on his dresser, so Tom More sees the joy to be found in living: "After all, why not live? Bad as things are still when all is said and done, one can sit on a doorstep in the winter sunlight and watch sparrows kick leaves" (97).

Tom More's honest response to the natural world indicates a reverence for Creation which Gabriel Marcel considers part of the Creator's plan: "My deepest and most unshakable conviction—and if it is heretical, so much that the worse for orthodoxy—is, that whatever all the thinkers and doctors have said, it is not God's will at all to be loved by us *against* the Creation, but rather glorified *through* the Creation and with the Creation as our starting point (*BH* 135). Once More, like Coleridge's Ancient Mariner, contemplates simple creatures and finds them beautiful, his salvation is possible, if only he will abandon the lapsometer. Making good on his decision to live, More sticks his bleeding wrists into his armpits and goes to his friend, Max Gottlieb, to have them sutured.

After this suicide attempt, More commits himself to the Acute Ward of the Fedville Hospital, and here the intersubjective alternatives to the lapsometer are powerfully presented. In the narrow world of the hospital, Tom More discovers both a sense of community and the possibility of communication: "Here I spent the best months of my life. . . . Here in the day room and in the ward we patients came to understand each other as only fellow prisoners and exiles can. Sane outside, I can't make head or tail of people. Mad inside, we signaled each other like auctioneers. . . . I listened and watched. Outside there is not time to listen" (105). Significantly, the intersubjective act of naming is stressed in the hospital scenes. First there is More's memory of feeling so bad that "I groaned aloud an Old Testament lamentation AAAAIEOOOOOW! to which responded a great silent black man sitting next to me on the blocky couch: 'Ain't it the truth though'" (105). And he credits Max Gottlieb with saving his life twice, "Once the night before by suturing my arteries. The next morning by naming my terror, giving it habitation . . . naming it with ordinary words, English common nouns" (109). So important was Max's naming act that More remembers Dr. Gottlieb's every gesture:

> Max smiling and spreading the skirts of his immaculate white coat and saying only, "Dr. More is having some troublesome mood swings. . . ." And all at once it, the terror, had a habitation and name—I was having "mood swings," right, that's what they were— and the doctors nodded and smiled and moved to the next bed. And suddenly the morning sunlight became just what it was, the fresh lovely light of morning. The terror was gone (110).

Just as the ordeal to which he subjected his body when he cut his wrists allowed More to discover the beauty of the Creation represented in sunlight, so Max's intersubjective naming of his dis-ease restores the morning sunlight so that Tom More can see and appreciate it; grace is manifested in the ordinary world around him.

At this lowest point of his life, More meets Ellen Oglethorpe, the nurse who takes care of him. Ellen enters More's life literally at the eleventh hour, when she is most needed: "A bad night it had been, my wrists bandaged and lashed to the rails, crucified. . . . Miss Oglethorpe, a handsome strapping nurse . . . came on at eleven and asked me what I wanted. 'I want you, Miss Oglethorpe. You are so beautiful and I need you and love you'" (109). Although

More's reaching out to Ellen here is sexual, at least he acknowledges and expresses need for another person.

In the Acute Ward, More has an insight about the creation, God, and our true status in the world as incarnated beings:

> Later, lust gave way to sorrow and I prayed, arms stretched out like a Mexican, tears streaming down my face. Dear God, I can see it now, why can't I see it other times, that it is you I love in the beauty of the world and in all the lovely girls and dear good friends, and it is pilgrims we are, wayfarers on a journey, and not pigs, nor angels (109).

Although More promptly loses this ability to see that it is God he loves and that the individual is properly Marcel's *homo viator* and neither angel nor beast, he *does* see clearly here, and the outcome of the novel is prepared for. The way of intersubjectivity, of naming and love, is thus *possible* for Tom More. When he leaves the hospital the following May, however, he turns his back on "my old friends and fellow madmen" (105) and promptly returns to his lapsometer, still convinced that with his gadget he can cure humankind's spiritual problems. The first thing More does is to go to the Little Napoleon tavern where he places a call to Osaka Instruments in Japan to order the first 100 lapsometers. This telephone call initiates the action which concerns the remainder of the novel. By choosing to put his faith in his own invention and turning away from the insights of the hospital, Tom More shows that he does not yet understand the Biblical injunction which echoes throughout the novel: "Physician, heal thyself" (20, 74, 215, 337).

Even if we allow More his madness and assume that once Art Immelmann adds the "differential stereotactic emission ionizer" to the lapsometer, More can "treat" as well as diagnose metaphysical uneasiness, the lapsometer is still worthless since its treatments wear off in a matter of minutes (211) and are "without lasting benefit" (199). In fact, judging by the treatment that More gives his antagonist, Dr. Buddy Brown, the effect lasts only a few minutes. Although Dr. Brown submits himself to a lapsometer reading, he makes fun of More and his invention: "Dr. More is going to diagnose me. . . . He is going to measure, not my blood alcohol, but my metaphysical status" (226). After More takes a reading and administers "moderate inhibitory dosages over the frontal cerebrum," Buddy continues to mock him: "Is that all, Doctor. . . . How is my metaphysical ontology? Or is it my ontological metaphysics?" (226).

Far from putting the broken self back together, the lapsometer seems to be no more than a portable Skinner Box, providing exactly the kind of reconditioning, numbing treatment which More himself has refused. When Max Gottlieb urges him to return to the hospital where his guilt could be conditioned away in the Skinner box, More refuses Max's offer, because he realizes that he *needs* the guilt if he is ever to repent. If his guilt were conditioned away, More explains to Max, "I'd really be up a creek" (118). The lapsometer, too, will numb the pain of the unnameable self, and thus prevent a person from taking steps toward the healing of the soul. The lapsometer anesthetizes exactly those centers of self which must be heard from if real changes are to occur. Tom More understands this, if he would only think, because of his experience with Max and the stand he has taken against behaviorism. But More is drunk, he has been given a lapsometer treatment by Art Immelmann, and he is so caught up in belief in his invention that he cannot see that it is just another mechanical device, not the "caliper of the soul" that he imagines.

If the lapsometer has any potential at all, it is only as a diagnostic tool in the naming of the problem, as More indicates in the case studies of his first two patients, P.T. Bledsoe and Ted Tennis. More notes that both men responded to having certain areas of their brains "touched" by the lapsometer's probes: "When I touched [Ted Tennis]—strange but this happened earlier with P.T. Bledsoe—he already seemed better" (34). Naming and touching could be carried out without the lapsometer; in fact it seems to be the touch that is most soothing. Human touch is a great comfort because it serves to remind abstracted persons that they are incarnated beings. As Dr. More notes: "Who of us now is not so strangely alone that it is the cool clinical touch of the stranger that serves best to treat his loneliness" (34).

The climactic scene in the Pit where Dr. More meets his antagonist, Dr. Brown, over the fate of a Mr. Ives, whom Brown wants to send to a euthanasia facility, serves to emphasize the problems that are rampant in this "broken world." The potential for abuse of the lapsometer is graphically presented as Art Immelmann distributes lapsometers to members of the audience, and More's colleagues fall lustfully all over each other. The scene also serves as a model for what will happen if individual beings are seen as problems to be solved rather than presences to be encountered.

As Marcel argues in *The Mystery of Being*, unless its proper weight is restored to ontology, unless the mysterious nature of Being is acknowledged, and the human person is seen as a being who is connected in an intersubjective network to other beings ("thous") and to Being (God, the "absolute Thou"), then respect for life will completely vanish from the world, which will become a world given over to death. If human beings are evaluated in terms of their functions, then human life will lose its value. Marcel argues that ultimately the reduction of the human being to machine leads to fanaticism of various kinds:

> *The less men are thought of as beings in the sense which we have already tried to define, the stronger will be the temptation to use them as machines which are capable of a given output;* this output being the only justification for their existence, they will end by having no other reality. There lies a road which runs straight to the forced labor camp and the cremation oven (*MB* 2: 165. Italics in original).

Or, in the case of Percy's Mr. Ives, the road leads to the Happy Isles of Georgia, a pleasantly named facility where pleasant deaths are induced. Mr. Ives has demonstrated antisocial behavior, he has refused to participate in the standard recreational activities for senior citizens, and he has resisted being conditioned in the Skinner box. Dr. Brown, therefore, believes Ives must be shuffled off to the Separation Center. In the behaviorist paradise of *Love in the Ruins*, good environments are defined, and people are expected to make their choices from goods which have been established for them by others. Mr. Ives, however, has found something valuable to do with what remains of his life: deciphering the Ocala frieze, an artifact from the proto-Creek culture. All Mr. Ives wants is to be left alone so that he can work on his scholarship, to be allowed not to participate in activities planned by others for his "happiness."

When Mr. Ives tells the story of his scholarship, it is clear that he is not an old duffer who will not cooperate, but a true searcher (*homo viator*) who wants to pursue his work. When the Director questions him about his antisocial behavior, Mr. Ives responds: "Doctor, how would you like it if during the most critical time of your experiments with the Skinner box that won you the Nobel Prize, you had been pestered without letup by a bunch of chicken-shit Ohioans? Let's play shuffleboard, let's play granddaddy golf, Guys and Gals à go-go" (231–32).

When someone like Mr. Ives fails to conform in this world, the problem is permanently solved at the euthanasia facility. At the end of *The Mystery of Being*, Marcel notes that although life is increasingly devalued, some sanctity remains: "It seems, at least as far as man is concerned, that even if life is weakened and in a way degraded, it must still retain a certain character of sacredness; otherwise there would be no reason for doubting the legitimacy of the treatment which supporters of euthanasia claim they may apply to incurables" (*MB* 2: 182). Mr. Ives represents us all. If the individual is not free to act as a subject, then the individual and the world are doomed. Life in the modern world, as Marcel argues, "has become more and more widely looked upon as a sort of worthless phenomenon, devoid of any intrinsic justification . . . subject to countless interferences which in a different metaphysical context would have been considered sacrilegious" (*MB* 2: 166). The euthanasia center in *Love in the Ruins* awaits us if death becomes our greatest good, because we may become consigned to death "without the power to resist the mesmeric power which death exerts over the man who has come to look on it as the final word" (*MB* 2: 167).

If humans are treated as mechanisms—as they are by both Tom More and his associates, the behaviorists—the world that Marcel imagined where intersubjectivity is replaced by objective-empirical approaches to humans has come into being: "In a world in which the arid influence of technique seems to prepare the radical disappearance of intersubjective relations, death would no longer be a mystery, it would become a raw fact like the dislocation of some piece of mechanism" (*MB* 2: 169). In a broken world where death becomes "raw fact," there develops a perverse "will for de-creation" which Marcel fears may become the dominant mode of human behavior (*MB* 2: 170). In words that Tom More would do well to heed, Marcel comments on the "blind powers" that have been loosed upon the world: "While we must not be too hasty in saying that these powers are human in essence, we must at least confess that even if they are not 'of man,' even if they are for example devilish, they have enlisted on their side instincts and passions which are indeed ours" (*MB* 2: 188–89). Art Immelmann, the resident devilish power in *Love in the Ruins*, makes exactly the same point when More accuses him of causing chaos with the lapsometer. Art defends himself: "Doc, we operate on a cardinal principle, which we never violate. We never 'do' anything to anybody. We only help people do what they want to do" (363). Without Tom More's full cooperation, in other words, Immelmann is powerless.

When Immelmann offers Ellen Oglethorpe a job as his traveling secretary, however, Tom finally defies the devil. By acting to save Ellen, he chooses one woman from the three he has stashed away at the Howard Johnson's motel. Of all Percy's female characters, Ellen is the least developed. She is more important for what she represents, old-fashioned strict Presbyterian morals, than for who she is.[10] Ellen is there for Tom More during all of the present action of the novel. She serves him as secretary and nurse, encouraging him to devote himself to his work, frowning on his constant drinking, taking care of him, trying to keep track of him. Her devotion to More argues her love for him. When More finally tires of dealing with the devil, Ellen is there to take him home.

More's relations with both Lola Rhoades, with whom he made love the previous Christmas eve—"One night I sang between her knees like an antique cello . . . A perfect encounter, but it is not to be thought that we could repeat it" (176)—and with Moira Schaffner, his "love from Love" who works at the Masters-and-Johnson-like Love Clinic, where orgasms are electronically recorded and charted, are inauthentic. With Lola the cellist, More enters Kierkegaard's realm of the musical-erotic; with Moira, he plays courtly love games, preparing a room for her at the deserted Howard Johnson's motel.

More's whole relationship with Moira, in fact, involves an impersonation, a devious constitution of himself that he has pre-pared as·carefully as he has prepared the bowerbird's nest in the deserted Howard Johnson's so that they can have a "trysting place" (73). The childlike Moira, "tapping her hard little fingernail on her tooth," asks him questions that beg for approval, "Do you like my hair long?" (259). It is Moira's childish profligacy that causes More's anger: "I can't understand how Moira can hold herself so cheaply. Why doesn't she attach the same infinite values to her favors that I do? With her I feel like a man watching a child run around with a forty-carat diamond. Her casualness with herself makes me sweat" (261).

Sharply contrasted to Moira, who holds herself cheap, is Ellen Oglethorpe, who is all business. In his initial descriptions of his three "girls," More explains that he sees both Lola and Moira romantically, whereas "Ellen Oglethorpe appears in my mind as in fact she is, a stern but voluptuous Presbyterian nurse, color high in her cheeks, eyes bright with disapproval" (14). More constantly notices Ellen's eyes which are "blue as Lake Geneva," (30, 261, 318, 345), an appropriate simile since the city is associated with the founder of Presbyterianism, John Calvin.[11] Ellen combines the mothering which More requires from Lola Rhoades and the child that he sees in Moira.

The child of Presbyterian missionaries, raised by an aunt who has urged her to save herself for her husband, Ellen does not fit well into More's plans to live with three women while revolution swirls around them. More realizes that Ellen may very well object to his plans, peculiar times or no:

> The question is: if worst comes to worst, what is the prospect of a new life in a new dead world with Lola Rhoades, to say nothing of Moira Schaffner and Ellen Oglethorpe. . . . Vines sprout in the plaza now. Fletcher Christian began a new life with three wives on faraway Pitcairn, green as green and unhaunted by old Western ghosts. I shall be happy with my three girls. Only Ellen, a Presbyte-rian, may make trouble (46).

Ellen would certainly never go along with More's plan to have three wives. Rather than remain with him unless he needs her, she prefers to take a job with Art Immelmann. Ellen's very presence in the motel reveals the love nest More has built for Moira for what it is: "[Ellen] lies on the bed, throwing the tufted chenille spread over her crossed ankles. How ill the chenille suits her! I blush at my summer's effort of fitting out this room as a trysting place. How shabby Ellen makes it all seem!" (336).

Ellen urges More to keep on with his work, offering, "I'll help you. We'll do it" (365). Her offer of herself and her use of the pronoun "we" apparently bring More to another moment of realization. He tells Ellen that he is not going back to his old inauthentic life: "I think of my old life: waking up Monday Tuesday Wednesday as not myself, breakfast on Tang and terror in the 'enclosed patio', Thursday, Friday afternoons a mystery of longing. My old life was a useless longing on weekdays, World War I at night, and drunk every weekend" (365–66).

When Art Immelmann reappears, Ellen offers to go to Copenhagen in More's place. Her offer, together with his recent memory of his daughter Samantha's warning him not to lose his faith, compel More to act at once. After realizing that he has been "feasting on death" (374), More turns toward life and utters a spontaneous prayer that banishes his personal devil: "*Sir Thomas More, kinsman, saint, best dearest merriest of Englishmen, pray for us and drive this son of a bitch hence*" (364). By asking St. Thomas More to intercede for him, More demonstrates what Marcel calls "the purest form of invocation—prayer—embodied imperfectly in the uttered word" (*CF* 32). According to Marcel, this kind of spontaneous prayer provides "a kind of inner transfiguration, a mysterious influx, an ineffable peace" (*CF* 32).

By choosing Ellen and rejecting Immelmann's offer of fame and the Nobel Prize, More opens himself to the workings of grace. Although More's prayer may be little more than a last ditch effort to save himself and Ellen, it is efficacious. Art Immelmann vanishes in a puff of smoke, and More is free to go home with Ellen:

> Art disappears into the smoke swirling beyond the bunker.
> "Now what?" asks Ellen.
> "I think I'll have a drink."
> "No, you won't. Let's go home," she says, spitting on me and smoothing my eyebrows (377).

The epilogue of *Love in the Ruins* is set on Christmas Eve, five years after the Christmas Eve of More's suicide attempt. Tom and Ellen have married and have two children, Meg and Tom Jr. The world has gone on with few changes other than who is in power. The Bantu revolution of five years ago failed; however, Paradise Estates is now 99 percent black because oil was discovered in Honey Swamp, and the blacks have bought out the whites. Tom and Ellen live in the old Slave Quarters, and Tom ekes out a happy life by seeing patients and running a "fat clinic" for the ladies at the Bantu country club.

The novel which began with Tom More looking out over the cloverleaf of an unnamed interstate highway, carbine across his lap, "waiting for the end of the world" (3), ends with a chastened More "hoeing collards in my kitchen garden" and "waiting and listening and looking at my boots" (381). An atmosphere of peace and calm, which contrasts sharply with the agitation of the events in July 1983, pervades the epilogue. Watching Ellen stirring grits as he rests with his back against a warm brick wall, More contemplates his new life. His practice has fallen off, but his health is better. He has not had a drink for six months, not because he has totally reformed but because "Ellen would kill me" (390). The most notable change is Tom More's sense of there being world enough and time. The frantic days of July 1–4 are over, and More comments on his new situation: "Strange: I am older, yet there seems to be more time, time for watching and waiting and thinking and working. All any man needs is time and desire and the sense of his own sovereignty. . . . I am a poor man but a kingly one" (382). Five years earlier, More felt that he had time for watching and waiting only when he was in the Acute Ward of the Fedville Hospital.

Gone from the Epilogue are the many references to More's attempt to see himself as Don Juan and to arias from *Don Giovanni* which occur in the novel proper. In their place is a proliferation of references to the historical Thomas More, humanist, author of *Utopia*, Lord Chancellor under Henry VIII, and martyr because of his refusal to sign the Oath of Supremacy. Tom More's identification with Sir Thomas More is illustrated by Tom's quoting him— "Knowing, not women, said Sir Thomas, is man's happiness"

(383)—and by several allusions, direct and indirect, to St. Thomas More's life and works. Describing Ellen, More says, "In my second wife I am luckier than my kinsman Thomas More. For once I have the better of him. His second wife was dour and old and ugly. Mine is dour and young and beautiful. Both made good wives" (384).

William Roper's *The Life of Sir Thomas More* provides the source of a number of the echoes that Percy sets reverberating throughout the epilogue. During the 14 months that Sir Thomas More was incarcerated in the Tower of London before his execution, he was comfortable enough since he was allowed books, writing materials and his personal servant. Roper stresses the additional comfort that More gained from the many visits of his eldest child, Meg, who was his favorite. Speaking of his imprisonment during one of Meg's visits, More tells his daughter:

> I believe, Meg, that they that have put me here ween they have done me a high displeasure. . . . I find no cause, I thank God, Meg, to reckon myself in worse case here than in my own house. *For me thinketh God maketh me a wanton, and setteth me on His lap and dandleth me.*[12]

Percy transforms the final sentence to its twentieth century equivalent and puts the words in Tom More's mouth. The love of a transcendent Father is richly evoked as Tom More remarks: "Poor as I am, I feel like God's spoiled child" (383). In the sixteenth century, the noun *wanton* referred to a child who was spoiled by overindulgence. The verb *dandle* meant to bounce a child gently up and down. Allowing for changes in the language in the more than 400 years separating the lives of Sir Thomas More and his fictional relative, we have the same simile. Thomas More in the Tower, knowing the consequences of defying his sovereign, felt at peace with himself and with his God. An abundance of grace allowed him to see God as a loving father who doted on him. The protagonist of *Love in the Ruins* also feels indulged, although he has very few material possessions. So poor is Tom More that the purchase of Ellen's Christmas present, a $603.95 king-size bed, wipes out a whole year's savings (391). But More takes great pleasure in the ordinary pleasures of his life, the bed, his new boots and common fare for meals—"grits and bacon and corn sticks" (384).

On Christmas Eve, More goes to confession for the first time in 11 years. Although he confesses his sins to Father Smith, More does not at first feel contrition. When he tells Father Smith that he is sorry "for not being sorry" (398), his words again echo those of his kinsman saint. In *Epigrammata*, Sir Thomas More wrote: "I counsel him that cannot be sad for his sin, to be sorry at the least that he cannot be sorry."[13] The Church's view of human nature is made clear in the epilogue of the novel. When Tom More seeks help from Father Smith to deal with his constant longings for other women and for alcohol, Father Smith reminds More: "That's the nature of the beast" (398). More needs to come to grips with the fact that longing, always wanting more, is part of what makes him human. The part of him that continues to work on the lapsometer, which he still believes will work, "if I can just get it right" (382) and that continues to hope that with his invention he can restore wholeness to a broken world, is argument enough for the positive benefits of longing.

Father Smith's advice to More points him toward other people as solutions to his problems. He suggests that More might consider an organization such as Alcoholics Anonymous: "For your drinking you might find it helpful, at least it is in my case, to cast your lot with other drunks" (399). Reminding Tom that there are more important things than his own longing to occupy his attention, Father Smith counsels More to reach out and become more available to others:

> Meanwhile, forgive me but there are other things we must think about: like doing our jobs, you being a better doctor, I being a better priest, showing a bit of ordinary kindness to people, particularly in our own families. . . . doing what we can for our poor unhappy country—things which, please forgive me, sometimes seem more important than dwelling on a few middle-aged daydreams (399).

Father Smith's words have definite Marcellian overtones as he directs More's attention away from the wound of self and toward others. In *The Mystery of Being*, Marcel defines all sin as "the act of shutting oneself in on oneself or of taking oneself as the center" (*MB* 2: 203), which is exactly what More has been doing. Father

Smith directs More's attention to the world of others, specifically to his own family, and suggests that although longing will continue, More's energy should be directed outward rather than wasted on what Marcel calls the "idolatry of self" (*HV* 20).

What Father Smith recalls More to is, in simple terms, a sense of his vocation. Father Smith's words are an invocation to which Tom More responds. More's immediate contrition—"'You're right. I'm sorry,' I say instantly, scalded" (399)—indicates that Marcel's sense of the vocation as a call that must come both from without and from *within* is operating here, because if the priest's words did not strike a cord in More, he would not respond so quickly with real contrition. Marcel says that vocation "is in reality a call. . . . It depends, in fact, on me whether the call is recognized as a call, and, strange as it may seem, in this matter it is true to say that it comes both from me and from outside me at one and the same time" (*HV* 23).

Tom More's movement from self-centeredness and self-absorption toward Ellen, and then five years later toward God, results finally in a tentative commitment to the larger community. After mass, Victor Charles announces that he plans to run for the U.S. Congress and asks More if he will be his campaign manager, explaining: "I got the Bantu vote. They've fallen out with each other and are willing to go with me. Chuck Parker's helping me with the swamp people. Max is working on the liberals. Leroy Ledbetter's got the peckerwoods. You could swing the Catholics" (401). Former enemies have found a compromise candidate in Victor Charles. Perhaps there is hope for America after all. By agreeing to become Victor's campaign manager, More embraces the idea that we may be able to solve some of our problems in the political arena if we make human community the focus of our activity. By opening himself to intersubjective service to the society, More fulfills the pattern which results, in Marcel's view, when persons reach their fullness by moving out from themselves: "Person—engagement—community—reality: there we have a sort of chain of notions which, to be exact, do not really follow each other by deduction . . . but of which the union can be grasped by an act of the mind" (*HV* 22). According to Marcel, when a person encounters others and treats them as "thous," then community is possible, and this kind of community, based on intersubjectivity, defines reality and creates a new world.

In the last scene of the novel, Tom More is at home, barbecuing in his sackcloth. By repenting and wearing on his body the outward signs of his inner contrition, sackcloth and ashes, More silently acknowledges the Church's authority to "treat" in metaphysical matters such as the sinful nature of human beings; he therefore assents to Marcel's assertion that "sin cannot be dealt with by any form of science, but only by the supernatural action of grace" (*BH* 191). Even in his sackcloth, More is a happy man:

> I'm dancing around to keep warm, hands in pockets. It is Christmas Day and the Lord is here, a holy night and surely that is all one needs.
>
> On the other hand I want a drink. Fetching the Early Times from a clump of palmetto, I take six drinks in six minutes. Now I'm dancing and singing old Sinatra songs and the *Salve Regina*, cutting the fool like David before the ark (402).

This passage echoes those in which More has remembered his joy after going to mass with Samantha, but there is a change in his choice of songs. Gone are the arias from *Don Giovanni*—"Finch 'han dal vino" (13) and "Là ci darem" (280) which More sang five years ago. Now he sings the song St. Thomas More mentioned when pondering what would become of his family after he resigned as Lord Chancellor. When they could no longer afford even the cheap food available at Oxford, the historical More hoped that "then may we yet with bags and wallets go a-begging together, and hoping that for pity some good folks will give their charity at every man's door to sing *Salve Regina*, and so still keep company merrily together."[14]

It is clear that Tom More has become more like his famous forebear. Although he does not seem aware of it, More is himself the man whom he hopes he might someday treat with his lapsometer, a man "who will walk into my office as ghost or beast or ghost-beast and walk out as a man, which is to say sovereign wanderer, lordly exile, worker and waiter and watcher" (383). If all goes well, Dr. Tom More will return to the work he is intended to do as a physician, to diagnose and treat the diseased body when his knowledge allows him to do so; and as for the rest, to be content to lay his hands on in comfort when the dis-ease goes beyond that which can be empirically known. Spiritual problems need the kind of spiritual treatment that only the Church can provide: contrition, confession, repentance and absolution.

"Lancelot"

The Nadir of Intersubjectivity

*L*ancelot, Percy's fourth novel, is his most unremittingly bleak.
For the first time, Percy clearly presents a model of what the
world would be like without intersubjectivity. The protagonist,
Lancelot Andrewes Lamar, is a middle-aged lawyer who has been
confined to the Center for Aberrant Behavior in New Orleans after
a fire at his ancestral home, Belle Isle. Lance's "aberrant behavior"
includes murder and arson, but his chief sin has been his rejection of
the intersubjective world of others. Marcel's admonition that all sin
is "the act of shutting oneself in on oneself or of taking one's own
self as a center" surely applies to Lancelot, who, in the course of his
long monologue, reveals himself to be, like Hawthorne's young
Goodman Brown, the chief horror of the tale he tells (*MB* 2: 203).
For five days beginning on November 1, All Saints' Day, Lancelot
tells his story to a boyhood friend, Harry Percy, now called by his
religious name of John.[1] Father John's current position at the Center
is not clear, and we have only Lance's statement that he may be
both priest and psychiatrist: "Are you a psychiatrist or a priest or a
priest-psychiatrist? Frankly you remind me of something in between, one of those failed priests who go into social work or
'counseling'. . . . If you're a priest why don't you wear priest
clothes instead of those phony casuals?"[2]

Perhaps the best way to understand the relationship which develops between Lancelot and John during the course of the novel is to
look at the recurring mirror metaphor, strongly present in the
opening sections. Percy has frequently used the image of the mirror
to talk about language. For example, in *The Message in the Bottle*, he

refers often to the intersubjective act of naming as it binds people
together with a common language. To describe the mysterious
nature of language and how hard it is to see what language does,
Percy writes: "Language is the very mirror by which we see and
know the world and it is very difficult to see the mirror itself, how
curiously wrought it is."[3] In "Naming and Being," Percy says,
"Trying to penetrate the act of naming is like trying to see a mirror
while standing in front of it."[4]

The mirror metaphor is useful in understanding Lancelot's relationship with John because each man provides a mirror in which the
other may come to see himself. Lancelot tells John how, a little over
a year ago, he caught sight of what he at first thought was a man as
he left the dining room at Belle Isle and walked through a darkened
parlor:

> I forgot to tell you another thing that happened in the parlor, a small
> but perhaps significant thing. . . . as I crossed the room to the
> sliding doors, something moved in the corner of my eye. It was a
> man at the far end of the room. He was watching me. He did not
> look familiar. There was something wary and poised about the way
> he stood, shoulders angled, knees slightly bent as if he were prepared
> for anything. He was mostly silhouette but white on black like a
> reversed negative. . . . There was a sense about him of a vulnerabil-
> ity guarded against, an overcome gawkiness, a conquered frailty. . . .
> Then I realized it was myself reflected in the dim pier mirror (63–64).

This unexpected glimpse of himself tells Lance far more than he can
see when he looks directly into his shaving mirror a few minutes
later. The direct look reveals only his own unformulable self:
"Looking at oneself in a mirror is a self-canceling phenomenon.
Eyes looking into eyes make a hole which spreads out and renders
one invisible. I had seen more of myself in that single glimpse of a
ghostly image in the pier mirror, not knowing it was I" (64). The
unexpected privileged view of himself, an objective view, allowed
Lancelot to briefly see himself as he appeared to others. We remember Marcel's and Percy's assertion that individuals must turn to the
"other" in order to have their own being affirmed. The "dim pier
mirror" provides a paradigm for the relationship between Lancelot
and John. John comes to see himself in the distorted mirror of his
old friend's tale. And Lance, as well, sees himself in John, as he says

during John's second visit: "When I saw you yesterday; it was like seeing myself" (53).

In *Lancelot*, Percy makes his first attempt at portraying both sides of an intersubjective relationship—something he will return to, with greater success, in *The Second Coming*. The pattern is not yet complete here, though, so we must be careful to notice the signs that indicate a great change in John. In an interview, Percy describes John as "a rather shadowy priest, who is kind of the mirror image of Lancelot."[5]

Like other priests who populate Percy's novels, Father Boomer in *The Last Gentleman* and Father Smith in *Love in the Ruins*, Father John is a "weary, flawed man, a wayfarer. . . . who has been sent as yet another replacement into hostile territory."[6] Lancelot's cell in the Center for Aberrant Behavior serves temporarily as a refuge for Lance and John, a haven from the world which has overcome them both. The narrow view from Lancelot's cell represents Lance's madness and the limited nature of his vision, yet it will be the very view that the priest needs to see. John discovers during the course of his visits what he might not have learned on many retreats: what the world would be like without Christian love and reconciliation, if all were rage and anguished hate. Lancelot's whole tale is like a reversed negative—"white on black"—for John, who must return to the only other available option, the Christian model, which argues that forgiveness, not retaliation, will lead to reconciliation and the resolution of differences.[7]

Lancelot clearly presents the radical need of two men for each other and the intersubjective relationship stripped to its essentials: two people and a world of objects and ideas to name. With intersubjectivity as our focusing point for *Lancelot*, we discover that the novel points in two directions.[8] Every word that Lancelot utters to his old friend—his description of his autonomous actions in the past, his mad plans for the New Order which he plans to lead in the future—undermines and denies the possibility of intersubjective love. Yet, at the same time, Lancelot's telling of the tale, his intersubjective naming act, is the very foundation of communion and world-sharing.

Because he understands dimly that he needs John, Lancelot uses a number of stratagems to ensure that John will return to his cell.

Initially, Lance insists upon their likenesses, reminding John of their shared past, of how in childhood they were "inseparable" (9). He also insists on their identity in the present, remarking that John seems abstracted, and repeating on a number of occasions, "something went wrong with you too" (11). Furthermore, he refers to the intersubjective moment which can be established by the look that passes between two people: "When our eyes met, there was the sense of our having gone through a great deal together, wasn't there?" (4). Lancelot also binds John to him by reminding him of his responsibility (as friend and priest) and by chiding John for abandoning him by going off to Biafra: "It was easier in Biafra, wasn't it, than in plain old Louisiana, U.S.A.?" (84); "Why did you leave twenty years ago? Wasn't Louisiana good enough for you? Do you think the U.S.A. needs you less than Biafra? I sometimes think that if you had been around to talk to . . ." (105–6). Here Lancelot breaks off, but his implication is clear. He wants John to feel that if he had been around to confide in, the catastrophe at Belle Isle might not have occurred. Thus, Lance tries to implicate John in the past, to make him partially responsible for those events.

Marcel's discussion of the privileged "other" to whom one may reveal one's sin is particularly useful in understanding John's relationship with Lancelot. In *Being and Having*, Marcel says that the only person who is qualified to show an individual the link between suffering and sin is someone who is willing to enter into that individual's sin:

> The man who from outside . . . draws my attention to the link between my suffering and my sin, needs to be inwardly qualified to carry out the act. He can be this only if he is himself entirely humble and offers himself as a sharer, as it were, in my sin. Perhaps he must even share in my suffering. In fact, he must become "another I." Insofar as he is pure and simple other, he cannot play this part. He is disqualified (*BH* 144).

Marcel goes on to suggest that this description of the "other" who shares in sin is especially important because it defines the "metaphysical relationship implied in priesthood" (*BH* 144). By sharing in another's sin, the priest takes a very different stand toward the sinner than would a moralist: "As soon as the priest begins to turn himself into a moralist, he denies himself as a priest" (*BH* 144). John, as we shall see, does provide Lancelot with "another I," humble enough to share in Lance's sin and suffering.

Silently listening for the most part—confining himself to questions that will encourage Lance to get on with his story—Father John agrees to serve as a priest in Marcel's sense, as one who participates in the sin. John is himself in need of another person: his problem with love and his near loss of faith bind him to Lancelot and make him a fellow sufferer. It is just as well that John does not attempt to argue with his old friend; such argument would be quite useless and would only aggravate Lance's antipathy to the Church which he vehemently attacks as having failed the world. The silent John is the ideal "other" to hear Lance's tale.

Lancelot prefers to call Father John "Percival" rather than by his religious name because the name ties John to the boyhood they shared. Although Lance calls him Percival, Father John reminds us of his religious name and his vocation by an action: he answers a call, an invocation from his old friend (4), when Lance sends for him. Although Lance observes John in the cemetery below his window apparently refusing when a woman asks him to say a prayer for the dead, it should be noted that John has not given up all his roles as priest, for he responds to this call.

Although the structure of the novel seems to indicate that we are to be most interested in Lance the monologist (after all, Father John's words are not recorded until the final two pages of the novel), the theme of intersubjectivity requires that we pay close attention to Percival/John. For Lance does not change during the course of telling his tale. His story told, he admits to John, "I feel nothing now except a certain coldness" (253). Lance remains obdurate even after he has drained some of the poison out of his system by naming it for John, by speaking it aloud in the presence of another. He lacks even Tom More's ability to feel sorry that he does not feel sorry: "No, no confession forthcoming, Father as you well know" (253). We may wait for Lance's salvation, but it does not occur. If we focus our attention on Lancelot, then, we will miss the change in John—the change which is this novel's main point.

Though it is impossible to tell what events have brought John to the Center for Aberrant Behavior, we can assume that whatever has gone wrong, John has suffered, and is suffering when the novel opens, some kind of crisis of faith, a dark night of the soul. Possibly he has become disillusioned as a result of the time he spent in Biafra. Certainly he is questioning his vocation after 20 years in the priesthood. Lancelot senses John's irresolution and goes for the jugular during their first meeting: "So something went wrong with you too. Or you wouldn't be here serving as assistant chaplain or substitute psychiatrist or whatever it is you're doing. A non-job. Are you in trouble? Is it a woman? Are you in love?" (11). What Lance calls John's "non-job" indicates the priest's ontological condition at the beginning of the novel. Like Tom More, who is on "patient-staff" status at the Fedville Hospital, John may have suffered some kind of breakdown. He may be another of Percy's ex-suicides. Unknowingly, Lance may have come close to naming John's problem, for certainly John's crisis of faith has to do with the love that he once felt for God and his fellow human beings which he now questions. Later, Lancelot challenges John again, this time reminding him of his unlikely conversion: "So wasn't it like your diving off the *Tennessee Belle* to go from unbeliever to priest, leapfrogging on the way some eight hundred million ordinary Catholics?. . . . And it didn't turn out too well, did it? Else why are you here? Something is wrong, isn't it? Have you lost your faith?" (61).

Whatever has brought John to the Center, his visits to Lance's cell provide an opportunity for him to see embodied in Lance's story the model of a world without Christian love and forgiveness. It seems likely, therefore, that Percy chose his epigraph from Dante's *Purgatorio* to indicate John's spiritual condition at the beginning of the novel, and that the pronoun *he*, which in the original refers to Dante, here refers to John, the troubled priest:

> He sank so low that all means
> for his salvation were gone,
> except showing him the lost people.
> For this I visited the region of the dead.[9]

The epigraph makes most sense if we see John as the one who has sunk low, whose soul, once committed to God, is in great danger. It is significant that John has a difficult time maintaining eye contact with Lance, preferring much of the time to look out the cell window to the cemetery where women are preparing the tombs for All Saints' Day. We are reminded that John looks away from Lance, avoids his gaze, by Lance's comment, "Ah, you smile your old smile. Yet you prefer to look at the cemetery" (10). Or a little later during the same visit: "Yet not even my sad case seems to interest you. Are you listening: What do you see down in the cemetery?" (22). Two conclusions may be drawn from what Lance says here. He is concerned that John may not be listening, and he is also aware that John avoids looking at him. Everything about John's body language indicates that he would like to escape these meetings. Apparently the actual dead are less threatening than the living dead man John sees before him—for Lancelot is, for all spiritual purposes, dead.

Until John's arrival, Lancelot has been living in self-imposed solitude for nearly a year, totally cut off from other people, the kind of alienation that Percy defines in "The Man on the Train" as "unspeakable."[10] Lancelot has been cut off from everyone except Anna, a catatonic patient in the next cell with whom he exchanges what he calls "messages" by tapping on the wall. Lancelot tells John that he does not know if their communication means anything. When Anna answers his two taps with two taps of her own, Lance admits, "It might have been an accident. On the other hand, it could have been true communication" (12). But taps, not certainly understood, do not create a language. For language to be effective, both people must agree on the meaning of words. For this sort of communication, Lancelot needs John. As Simone Vauthier points out, there is evidence that Lancelot has spoken with people on the staff at the Center, but that he has not revealed himself or his world to them.[11] Instead of communicating, Lancelot has apparently played games with the staff members and has said what he thought they wanted to hear. But there has been no genuine communication, no world-sharing. When Father John appears in his cell, however, Lancelot emerges from the unspeakability of alienation and tells his story to his old friend, realizing that John might have something to tell him, or that the mere journey back into the past, "kick[ing] through the ashes of Belle Isle" may provide a clue to what went wrong in his life (108).

Percy argues that two people naming the world together can create reality, a world that is intersubjectively theirs because each agrees to accept it, but only Lancelot speaks in this novel. John simply listens, apparently waiting until Lance vents all his spleen before he comments. Lance's world is a horrible place, one which has driven him to revenge, arson and murder, out of which comes more death—the death of his soul as well as the deaths of four people at Belle Isle. As the tale of his wife's adultery and his own revenge progresses, Lancelot becomes more vitriolic, his language more violent as he ferociously attacks an America which he compares to Sodom. Deranged and exhibiting certain symptoms of psychosis, Lancelot is engulfed in bitterness and hatred.

The telling of any story is by definition subjective, since the teller includes some details and omits others. Nonetheless, the addition of a listener who reacts to the story makes the experience intersubjective. Father John must agree to accept the names that Lance provides. According to Percy, the naming act is at the very heart of the intersubjective nature of language. Once one person names something for another person, and the two agree to call the object by a common name, they establish a world held in common under the auspices of language. Although Lancelot would prefer to approach the world on a dyadic level, choosing, for example, to see sexual intercourse as nothing more than molecules reacting with other molecules, John's very presence enlarges Lancelot's world. And John's active, though silent, rejection of much that Lancelot says keeps their relationship on a triadic level where meaning is always at issue.[12] By refusing with a look or gesture to accept something that Lancelot says, John recalls Lancelot to the intersubjective world of shared definitions and meanings.

Just as important as John's acceptance of Lancelot's definitions is his act of constantly returning Lancelot to the central question of the novel, a question asked lyrically in *Love in the Ruins*—"Love, where is love now?" (*LR* 136). If Lancelot and John are to share a world by naming it, they must first agree on the definition of love. Although none of John's words are recorded until the last pages of the novel, we can tell by Lancelot's responses that the priest continually asks questions. In response to John's reiterated question about Lance's wife Margot, "Did you love her?" (89, 90, 117, 118,

122, 254), Lancelot answers in similar ways: "But what is love?" (81); "Love. Hm. The older I get, the less I know about such large subjects" (89); "Did I love Margot? I'm not sure what you mean, what the word means, but it was good between us" (117); "Love her? I'm not sure what words mean any more, but I loved her if loving her is wanting her all the time" (119); "Did I love her? Why are you always asking about love?" (122). It is clear from Lance's responses that he does not share John's definition of love. For Lance love is *eros*, the possessing of a woman. As a result of John's constant questioning, Lancelot's definition, his naming act, comes to the fore. For Lance, love has only to do with sex, with Marcel's realm of Having. He cannot admit to any other kind of love. Lance finally loses patience and vehemently attacks the priest, who has continually asked him if he loved Margot: "Don't talk to me of love until we shovel out the shit" (179).

With this constant emphasis on love, it is interesting that Harry Percy has taken John as his religious name. On the second day that Father John comes to his cell, Lancelot comments: "John, a good name. But is it John the Evangelist who loved so much or John the Baptist, a loner out in the wilderness?" (10). Lancelot refers, of course, to two traditional figures of significance in the New Testament. Father John does embody aspects of the character of John the Baptist in that he is a loner and, as least as far as Lance is concerned, he may indeed be a voice crying in the wilderness. The figure of John the Evangelist provides a more complex comparison. Traditionally, John the Evangelist has been believed to be one of the twelve disciples and also the author of the fourth gospel, three epistles and the book of Revelation. Most Biblical scholars, however, dispute the notion that one man was responsible for filling all these roles. Lance's reference to "John the Evangelist who loved so much" clearly refers to the apostle John who leaned on Jesus's shoulder at the Last Supper, the one disciple who remained faithful and stood at the foot of the cross and to whom Jesus commended his mother. The Gospel of John, though perhaps not written by the apostle, is also important. Lewis Lawson suggests that Father John may have intended to model himself on this John the Evangelist, the author of the gospel that, more than any other, emphasizes the role of love in the Christian good news.[13] Since Lancelot's worldview is representative of what Percy calls "the Greco-Roman tradition," it is significant that the author of the Gospel of John attempted to make the good news acceptable to Greeks by identifying Christ with their own concept of *logos*.[14] The images suggested by the Book of Revelation, as well, should not be overlooked. Although the John who authored this chapter of the New Testament is not, according to most scholars, either the disciple John or the author of the fourth gospel, there has been a traditional linking of John the Evangelist to this book. In light of the secular apocalypse which Lance has already brought about at Belle Isle—and in light of the entirely apocalyptic worldview which we come to find in Lance—this association is an interesting one. God is not a part of Lancelot's apocalyptic worldview, whereas the Book of Revelation shows the overcoming of evil and persecution and the triumph of God. Father John, as he constantly speaks to Lance about love, may desire to bring something of God's love to this worldview.

The story Lancelot tells John reveals a life without love. With the exception of his boyhood friendship with John, Lancelot's life has been singularly lacking in any kind of intersubjective communion with others. Notably absent in Lancelot's account is any mention of familial love. His difficulties seem to have begun in early childhood. Memories of his mother, who may have had an affair with "Uncle Harry," and of his father, whom he describes as "a failed man who missed the boat all around but who knew how far away Arcturus was," haunt Lancelot (56).

His feelings for the members of his own family further illustrate the failure of intersubjective love in his life. Lancelot is the father of two children by his first marriage, and his second wife, Margot, also bore a child he believed to be his. He tells John of an unnamed son, currently a homosexual, whom he has not seen "since he quit college and went to live in a streetcar behind the car barn" (50). Of Lucy, the older daughter who lived with him at Belle Isle, Lance says, "We were not close," and he later reveals his own warped perspective when he describes Lucy as "a child whom voluptuousness had overtaken unawares. . . . This innocent voluptuousness was the sort . . . to inspire lewdness in strangers" (50, 136). He confesses to John that he did not love seven-year-old Siobhan even before he discovered that she was not his child: "Why didn't I love Siobhan when I thought she was my own child? Well, I suppose I 'loved' her. What is love? Why this dread coldness toward those closest to you and most innocent: Have families ever loved each other except when some dread thing happens to somebody?" (55). Lancelot also reveals his hatred of women and his obsession with their sexuality when he remarks that little Siobhan "liked to show her body" concluding that "she was as sexual a creature as her mother" (117). This "dread coldness" seems to summarize how he felt about his family. He retreated from them into the pigeonnier where he drank himself into a stupor every night. Now, he tries to make some sense of them retrospectively, but he is unable to understand anything about who they were or what they thought because he never really loved them or was available to them.

Lancelot's two marriages also reveal the failure of intersubjectivity in his life. His first wife, Lucy Cobb, he loved romantically. She was no more real to him than "a dream, a slim brown dancer in a bell jar spinning round and round in the 'Limelight' music of old gone Carolina long ago" (119). Although Lucy died young, she seems not to have been real enough even to suffer. Lancelot summarizes their life together: "We were married, moved into Belle Isle, had two children. Then she died. I suppose her death was tragic. But to me it seemed simply curious. How curious that she should grow pale, thin, weak, and die in a few months! Her blood turned to milk—the white cells replaced the red cells" (84). Lancelot saw Lucy not as an individual woman with a soul but as a body that contained blood cells that ran amuck. His point of view here is strangely detached.

Lancelot's relationship with his second wife, the lusty Margot, was no better, although Lance continually tries to convince himself and John that what they shared was "love." But his definition of love has nothing to do with creating a world in common with Margot. For Lancelot, love does not reach beyond physical presence; it was Margot's body he loved. Lancelot confounds Marcel's categories of Having and Being, finding in his second wife only an object to be possessed, not a woman to be loved. Lance explains that in the early days of the marriage he was consumed with erotic love. Then, something happened—the failure of the erotic to establish intersubjective communion, though Lance is unaware of that fact—and he began to drink. He became a poor lover, and he refers to his alcohol-induced impotence as his "secret wound," echoing Marcel's definition of the ego as "the wound I bear within me." Although Lance does not acknowledge his own responsibility for the failure of his marriage, his references to his heavy drinking explain Margot's loss of interest in him: "When I took to the bottle—a different love story—and became a poor lover, once again inattentive and haunted, she came to prefer restoration to love" (119).

Because Lancelot thinks of Margot as an object to be possessed and of orgasm as the only earthly infinity, he thinks he has the right to dispose of her when she betrays him sexually.[15] Here Marcel's argument that we can only dispose of that which we think of ourselves as *having* illuminates Lancelot's relationship with Margot. Caught up in desire, Lancelot is unable to transcend Marcel's realm of Having in order to enter the realm of Being. Therefore he has no definition of self apart from what he *has*. Marcel comments: "We are tempted to think that no longer having anything is the same as no longer being anything: and in fact the general trend of life on the natural level is to identify one's-self with what one has" (*BH* 84). Marcel also argues that total involvement with Having ultimately leads to an "alienation of the subject . . . in the face of the thing, whatever it may be" (*BH* 166). If Lancelot had been able to share in the realm of Being with Margot, if he had been able to love her instead of merely desiring her, then the tension between them could have been broken. But as long as only desire operates, intersubjective love is impossible. Marcel suggests that love is at the opposite pole from desire:

> Love, insofar as distinct from desire or as opposed to desire, love treated as the subordination of the self to a superior reality, a reality at my deepest level more truly me than I am myself—love as the breaking of the tension between the self and the other, appears to me to be what one might call the essential ontological datum. . . . love comes first (*BH* 167).

Both Lancelot's attraction to Margot and his fury when he discovers her infidelity are illustrations of his inhabiting Marcel's realm of Having. Father John must notice how frequently Lancelot refers to desiring and possessing Margot:

> There was a time just before and just after we were married when I could not not touch her. There was no getting enough of her (89).

> There was no other thought than to possess her, as much of her with as much of me and any way at all, all ways and it seemed for always (90).

> Love her? I'm not sure what words mean any more, but I loved her if loving her is wanting her all the time, wanting even the sight of her (118).

Because physical lovemaking allowed Margot and Lance their only point of contact and was the foundation of their marriage, Lancelot could not bear the thought of Margot with another man. He tells John that this thought is "unspeakable," and he tortures himself with thoughts of "her head turning to and fro in a way I knew only too well, her lips stretched, a little mew-cry escaping her lips" (16). He describes to John how he imagined himself a cuckold after his discovery that his daughter Siobhan's blood type did not match his. He compares himself to an astronomer who can see the end of the world in a misplaced dot in the heavens. Lancelot imagines how Margot must have looked making love to another man:

> Beyond any doubt she was both beside herself and possessed by something, someone? else. Such considerations have led me to the conclusion that, contrary to the usual opinion, sex is not a category at all. It is not merely an item on a list of human needs like food, shelter, air, but is rather a unique ecstasy, ek-stasis, which is a kind of possession (21).

Here Lancelot's scrambling of Marcel's realms of Having and Being is apparent. Woman, specifically Margot, is only an object, something to be possessed by man. In a revealing simile, Lance sees Margot as like the land, which can also be possessed, plowed and made to bear fruit: "Margot was life itself as if all Louisiana, its fecund oil-rich dark greens and haunted twilights, its very fakery and money-loving and comicalness, had all been gathered and fleshed out in one creature" (119).

Just as Lancelot's primary relationship to his world was one of

Having, so Margot's main interest came to be the accumulation of antiques and the restoration of Belle Isle. Margot filled her hours "pouring over old sketches, enlisting historians, importing Carrara marble carvers" (120). However, the realm of Having exerts its demands: as long as one's relationship to the world is defined by having, one must constantly have more. After Margot completed her restoration of Belle Isle, she decided it was time to have a child. She was interested, however, only in *having* a child, not in *being* a mother. The nurturing of her daughter Siobhan she left to her father, Tex, while she went off to study acting with Robert Merlin in order to *have* a career.

Caught up in their separate worlds of Having, Lance and Margot failed to enter each other's worlds, except in bed. It is significant that Lancelot, for all his desire to know for sure whether or not Margot was unfaithful, was never able to approach her through the intersubjective medium of language and ask her a direct question. Even in his penultimate encounter with Margot, he could not ask whether she had had lovers, and he asks John, "Why couldn't I ask her what I wanted to know?" (174). The intersubjective communion that language makes possible simply was not a part of their marriage. Margot herself was apparently vaguely aware that she was real to Lancelot only insofar as he could place her in a category, as she indicates in her last words: "That's what you never knew. With you I had to be either—or—but never a—uh—woman" (245). The two suppressed nouns here are *lady* and *whore*, the two designations that Lancelot has for women.

Lancelot explains to John the two important discoveries that he made when his "new life" began a year ago:

> A year ago (was it a year?) I made my two great discoveries: one, Margot's infidelity; two, my freedom. I can't tell you why, but the second followed directly upon the first. The moment I knew for a fact that Margot had been fucked by another man, it was as if I had been waked from a twenty-year dream. I was Rip Van Winkle rubbing his eyes. In an instant I became sober, alert, watchful. I could act (107).

In the light of intersubjectivity, the connection between Lancelot's two discoveries is clear. Since the relationship was based on physical attraction and desire rather than on love, Margot's giving her body to another man was the ultimate betrayal. Once the sexual connection was broken, Lancelot was free. He could then approach her infidelity not as a mystery in which he was himself involved (his drinking, his withdrawal, his impotence), but as a problem to be solved. He could abstract himself from their marriage and stand outside it.

After a ritual bath, Lancelot felt totally cut off from others and free to act. He tells John that he took pride in his newfound independence from drugs and in his alienation from the human community: "I stood up. Can a man stand alone, naked, and at his ease, wrist flexed at his side like Michelangelo's David, without assistance, without diversion, without drink, without friends, without a woman, in silence? Yes. It was possible to stand. Nothing happened" (66). He is, of course, wrong. When he resolved to take matters into his own hands, following a chivalric code of his own devising, totally cut off from any intersubjective love of the "other," he unleashed the violence and death-dealing which such a retreat invokes. Caring nothing for himself or others, his only emotion curiosity—"the worm of interest" (21, 27, 29, 32)—Lancelot became a tool of the destructive forces that he sees everywhere in contemporary America. At the end of the novel, Lancelot persists in seeing himself as cut off from any code other than his own: "I am my own instrument," he tells John (256).

Marcel warns that freedom and action cut off from any sense of responsibility for one's actions lead to anarchy. In *Being and Having*, Marcel first approaches the distinction between autonomy and freedom. Lancelot's concept of "freedom" is essentially the same as Marcel's "autonomy":

> Autonomy. . . . is the "by myself!" of the little child who is beginning to walk and rejects the hand outstretched to him. "I want to run my own life"—that is the radical formula of autonomy. It refers essentially to action and implies . . . the notion of a certain province of activity circumscribed in space and time (*BH* 132).

Much of what Marcel has to say in this journal entry is applicable to Lancelot's situation as he rejects communion with others and takes pride in his isolation. Because Lancelot sees others as objects and also as possessions over which he has control, he moves one step further and decides to dispose of them.

Lance's objective approach to his own situation is apparent in his envying the surety of science: "How happy scientists are! Why didn't we become scientists, Percival? They confront problems which can be solved. We don't know what we confront. Does it have a name?" (100). Although he seems here to indicate an awareness that there are mysteries in life, Lancelot would like to believe that relations between people are nothing more than a sequence of stimulus and response events such as those that can be observed in the laboratory. He would like to see Margot's adultery as nothing more than the interaction of molecules, as he tells John:

> Why did it become the most important, the sole obsession of my very life, to determine whether or not Margot slept with Merlin. . . . You tell me, you being the doctor-scientist and soul expert as well, merchant of guilt and getting rid of it and of sorting out sins yet knowing as well as I that it, her fornication, anybody's fornication, amounts to no more than molecules and little bursts of electrons along tiny nerves—no different in kind from that housefly scrubbing his wings under my hair (89).

Once one has come to the point of considering sexual intercourse as nothing more than the interaction of molecules, one has lost all intersubjectivity, considering the "other" not as subject, but as object. Seen objectively, as neurological events, Margot's fornication and the fly tickling the hair on Lancelot's arm are perhaps similar. Seen subjectively, however, there is all the difference in the world. Margot's infidelity was a betrayal of a relationship, and Lancelot cannot quite convince himself that it was no more than a molecular event.

In a disturbing passage near the end of the novel, however, Lancelot pushes this objective view of human behavior to its logical conclusion. If encounters between people are nothing more than neurological events, then anything is allowed. There is nothing to prevent the taking of another person's life, since cutting a throat is only an interaction between molecules. Lance describes to John how he felt as he cut Janos Jacoby's throat after finding him in bed with Margot: "Not even the knife at his throat seemed to make any difference. All it came down to was steel molecules entering skin molecules, artery molecules, blood cells" (254).

Lancelot approaches evil itself as if it were a problem to which he can find the solution. Unlike Tom More, who understands that "the mystery of evil is the mystery of limited goodness" (*LR* 45), Lancelot sees evil as a problem rather than as a mystery in which he is involved. In *Being and Having*, Marcel comments on the tendency of idealist philosophers to approach evil in this way:

> I am naturally inclined to consider evil as a disorder which I look into; I try to make out its causes, the reason for its existence, and even its hidden ends. . . . But evil simply recognized, or even contemplated, ceases to be evil *suffered*, in fact I think it simply ceases to be evil. I only really grasp it as evil in proportion as it touches me; that is, when I am involved in it. . . . Traditional philosophy has tended to reduce the mystery of evil to the problem of evil (*BH* 171–72).

Thus Lancelot is not only a thoroughgoing Gnostic as both Brooks and Lawson have suggested, but he is also like Marcel's idealist philosopher who separates himself from the human mystery in which he participates in order to study it and find a "solution" to it.[16] Lancelot confounds Marcel's categories of problem and mystery just as he does the realms of Having and Being. He cannot see that he himself is part of the mystery of evil because he does not believe in his own sin.

Lancelot's evolving fanaticism also has a direct connection to his fascination with Having. In *Being and Having*, Marcel discusses his belief that treating ideas and convictions as possessions can be dangerous:

> The more I treat my own ideas, or even my convictions, as something *belonging* to me—and so as something I am proud of as I might be proud of my greenhouse or my stables—the more surely will these ideas and opinions tend, by their very inertia . . . to exercise a tyrannical power over me; that is the principle of fanaticism in all its shapes. What happens in the case of the fanatic, and in other cases too, it seems, is a sort of unjustified alienation of the subject. . . . The ideologist is one of the most dangerous of all human types, because he is unconsciously enslaved to a part of himself which has

mortified, and this slavery is bound to manifest itself outwardly as tyranny (*BH* 166).

Just as Marcel has shown that a person who is caught up in possessing *things* may finally be possessed by the things owned, that "having" becomes a kind of slavery, he here argues that *ideas* may also take over and enslave the individual. Such appears to be the case with Lancelot Lamar.[17] Using his individual experience as a model, Lance announces his plans for the "new order" he intends to establish in the Shenandoah Valley as soon as he is released. These mad plans for a new order of society finally bring John, the silent listener, face to face with a choice between his faith and a mass movement of crazed individuals who act on their own definitions of right and wrong. Lance's neo-fascist order provides a negative image of the intersubjective community of believers which John as priest represents.

Lance's plans for what he variously calls a "new order," a "Third Revolution" (157) and a "New Reformation" (177) are based partially on the old chivalric code which he values, harking back to a time when he believes that men were men and women were either ladies or whores. Lance tells John that his new order will be totally secular. He expressly bans Christian love from his community, answering an apparent question from John with, "Then how shall we·live if not with Christian love? One will work and take care of one's own, live and let live, and behave with a decent respect toward others" (158). His alternative community is based on a radical "freedom" which allows all individuals to act for themselves. Although he admits that consensus has disappeared, Lance tells John that the members of his new order will recognize each other:

> We will know each other as gentlemen used to know each other—no, not gentlemen in the old sense—I'm not talking about social classes. I'm talking about something held in common by men, Gentile, Jew, Greek, Roman, slave, freeman, black, white, and so recognized between them; a stern code, a gentleness toward women and an intolerance of swinishness, a counsel kept, and above all a readiness to act, and act alone if necessary. . . . If one man is free to act alone, you don't need a society (157).

Here are all the elements of the world that Lancelot will substitute for the intersubjective community of believers. Significantly, Lancelot uses words that will remind John of Paul's words to the Galatians: "For as many of you as were baptized into Christ have put on Christ. There is neither Jew nor Greek, there is neither slave nor free, there is neither male nor female; for you are all one in Christ Jesus" (Galatians 3: 27–28).

But Lancelot will replace Christ at the center of the new order, and he imagines followers "who are strong and pure of heart, not for Christ's sake but for their own sake" (178). Lancelot advocates total anarchy, and John has in front of him the modern morality play of Lancelot's past actions at Belle Isle to demonstrate the end result of one man's acting alone in accordance with a code based on a readiness, even an eagerness, to act. John apparently reacts at this point, either by words or gesture, no doubt remembering that Lance's most recent refusal to tolerate the age has led to the murders at Belle Isle. Lance reassures him: "Actually, you don't have to worry. Killings will not be necessary" (159). But John, who has been listening patiently, is forewarned to heed the tale and not the teller (159). Killings were necessary one year ago at Belle Isle when Lance set out upon his old "new life."

The men of Lance's new order will have in common only an agreement that society is in dire straits and their determination to take matters into their own hands. There will be no community, no brotherhood, no forgiveness or reconciliation, no intersubjective world because God's love is not to be allowed in the new society. In stark contrast to the Christian order where "there is neither male nor female," women will be either ladies or whores and everyone will know the difference. There will be no room for complexities or ambiguities in human behaviour. Sitting in his cell, Lance turns his back on the human community, dreaming instead of a new world of absolutes, of clear and simple blacks and whites. Ultimatums will be issued whenever anyone steps out of line. As Lancelot confides to John, "Either one shakes hands with someone or one ignores him or one kills him. What else is there?" (149). When John asks Lancelot how women will fare under the new order, Lance responds, "Freedom? The New Woman will have perfect freedom. She will be free to be a lady or a whore" (179).

Lancelot further explains that he will be the ideal leader of this new order because he has two necessary qualities of leadership—conviction and freedom:

> The conviction: I will not tolerate this age. The freedom: the freedom to act on my conviction. And I will act. No one else has both the conviction and the freedom. Many agree with me, have the conviction, but will not act. Some act, assassinate, bomb, burn, etc., but they are the crazies. Crazy acts by crazy people. But what if one, sober, reasonable, and honorable man should act, and act with perfect sobriety, reason, and honor? Then you have the beginning of a new age. We shall start a new order of things (156).

In order not to be alone, Lance deludes himself into believing that there are "millions" who are eager to join his Third Revolution to save the United States from sexual sin. At one point, Lancelot appears delusional to the point of imagining marching men outside his window. He asks John, "Do you hear the sound of music far away? No? Perhaps I only imagined it. . . . But I swear I could hear the sound of young men marching and singing, a joyful cadenced marching song" (218). The only kind of community that Lance can imagine is one of an army on the move. This certainly does not represent a Marcellian view of community. In a discussion of Sartre's view of the "other," Marcel says that Sartre has no understanding of the "other" except as comrade in arms or work: "[T]he sense of community—the sense of forming part of a we-subject—is only experienced on such occasions as when a regiment is marching in step or a gang of workmen pulling together" (*PE* 74).

Lancelot's new order provides the completed mad model of intersubjectivity, with hate and violence at its core instead of love, with the human being the measure of all things instead of God, with action and violence as the prime modes of demonstrating that each person is autonomous, each person an instrument in a world gone crazy with lust and perversion. John reacts to Lance's descriptions of the Third Revolution by turning pale, and Lance comments, "You look stricken for the first time since you've been coming here" (160). When John appears in Lancelot's room the next day, he has abandoned his civilian dress and has put on his priestly vestments. Having been shown a world in which each man can act as he sees fit in order to uphold an ill-defined code of honor that seems to have mostly to do with punishing women, John must choose that other world of orthodox Christianity which promises redemption and reconciliation. He must counter Lance's hatred and bile with love. Following yet another diatribe from Lancelot, John turns pale, and Lance comments: "You are pale as a ghost. What did you whisper? Love? That I am full of hatred, anger?" (179).

Although John and Lancelot represent two diametrically opposed worldviews, they agree that a new beginning must be made (257). John's new beginning is to take a small parish in Alabama and become an ordinary priest again, his expectations about saving the world lowered. John will serve as one who is content to "watch and wait" for any signs of God's presence in the world. Meanwhile, he will be himself a sign, a vessel of God's grace for ordinary Buick dealers. John's willingness to accept the everyday world of sin in contemporary America indicates his having come to terms with his own spiritual crisis. Through listening to Lancelot's story and sharing in his sin, John has concluded that humankind stands in need of redemption. The alternative to an intersubjective community is clearly unacceptable.

Although Lance mocks John's plan to serve as a parish priest, he should appreciate John's new commitment, since earlier he had taken a different stand on the place of the church in the world: "I like your banal little cathedral in the Vieux Carré. It is set down squarely in the midst of the greatest single concentration of drunks, drugheads, whores, pimps, queers, sodomists in the hemisphere. But isn't that where cathedrals are supposed to be?" (23). Now, however, he dismisses John's rededication to his vocation as "more of the same" (257). What Lancelot fails to see is that his own "new life" will also be more of the same. After he reports his "good news" to John—that he has been found sane and is to be released—he tells the priest, "Then I shall pick up my little suitcase, which contains my worldly possessions, a change of underwear, one suit, socks, sweater, Bowie knife, and boots" (250). It does not bode well for Lance's new life that along with a few items of clothing, he intends to pack the Bowie knife he used to slit Janos Jacoby's throat, a knife so important to him that he went back to retrieve it from Belle Isle, burning his hands in the process. The headline that Lance recalls—SUFFERS BURNS TRYING TO SAVE WIFE (13)—turns out to be totally inaccurate. In one of the most chilling sections of the novel, Lance tells John what happened after he was blown out of the window by the explosion at Belle Isle:

> I stood up, for some reason put my hands in my pockets, and walked up the front steps as I had done ten thousand times before. The heat, carried away by the wind, was not great. . . . Most of the walls of the ground floor were down. There was no second floor.
> What did you say? How did I get burned?
> I had to go back to find the knife (246).

Unlike John's, Lancelot's entire worldview is apocalyptic, and completely secular. Unable to tolerate the age and to leave any intervention in the sinful progress of humankind to God, he decides to usher in the Last Days by becoming one of the signs that will mark the end of the world. John, however, will "watch and wait" for a sign, knowing that it may not come in his lifetime. He will not judge the world, nor will he tolerate it; rather he will live in the world as an instrument of God's love. Thus it is John who follows Scripture and Lance who violates it. After describing various signs which will accompany the Last Days, Jesus warns his disciples not to try to anticipate the end:

> But of that day or that hour no one knows, not even the angels in heaven, nor the Son, but only the Father. . . . Watch therefore—for you do not know when the master of the house will come, in the evening, or at midnight, or at cockcrow, or in the morning—lest he come suddenly and find you asleep. And what I say to you I say to all: Watch (Mark 13: 32, 35–37).

Even the deranged Lancelot is not beyond the redemptive power of love. As he rants about his plans for a new life in the Shenandoah Valley, his old friend, Percival, stands ready to offer Lancelot the forgiveness that he needs, to be John, the bearer of the good news of Christ's redemptive love. It is possible that even so great a sinner as Lancelot Lamar may be forgiven and returned to the human community. John himself is a changed man, as Lancelot notices—"I have a feeling that while I was talking and changing, you were listening and changing" (254). John is apparently willing to be the "other" that Lancelot so badly needs.

The very last word of this dark novel is a word of affirmation from the priest. When Lancelot announces that he has finally done with talking, he asks John if he has anything to tell him before he leaves. John responds, "*Yes*" (257). It is love that John wants to tell Lance about, his own love and God's. If Lancelot opens himself to the grace embodied in the one person with whom he has ever really shared himself, he may discover the kind of intersubjective love that will lead him to Marcel's "absolute Thou," whose representative John has rededicated himself to being.

"The Second Coming"

Intersubjectivity Achieved

Twenty years older than he was in *The Last Gentleman*, Will Barrett returns in *The Second Coming*.[1] During this long interval, Will was married and lived a reasonably good life in New York City; he has now inherited millions from his wife, Marion Peabody, who dies shortly before the novel opens. He has a grown daughter, Leslie, a born-again Christian who signs letters, "Yours in the Lord."[2] As the world defines success, Will Barrett has everything a man could hope for; he has even taken early retirement from his career as a lawyer, a freedom which allows him to spend much of his time playing golf. During a golf game, Jimmy Rogers remarks to Will: "You made it in the big apple, you married a nice Yankee lady who owns half of Washau County, you retired young, you came down here and you helped folks. . . . Now your lovely daughter is getting married. Joy and sorrow, that's life. But yours seems mostly joy" (69–70).

But Jimmy Rogers is mistaken; all is not well with Will Barrett. He has taken to falling down all over the golf course. Afflicted with recurring amnesiac spells in *The Last Gentleman*, Will Barrett now suffers from total recall, the intrusion on his consciousness of incidents from his past that makes it impossible for him to live in the present. There are two explanations for Will's "condition," the medical and the existential. Doctors at Duke University finally determine that his total recall results from "Hausmann's Syndrome," a condition which can be treated by giving Will the hydrogen ions that he lacks.[3] According to the experts, the petit mal seizures which periodically throw Will to the ground can be explained by a chemical imbalance. But Will's constant preoccupation with death places him squarely in the existential tradition, where, as Marcel points out, of all the future events that await an individual, only death is certain and inescapable. The realization of one's own approaching death can make one dizzy and cause despair.[4] J. Gerald Kennedy argues that Will's fainting spells are a classic Freudian syndrome, the result of Will's repression of a traumatic childhood memory of a hunting trip he took with his father.[5]

As Kennedy has observed, Will's loss of his wife Marion six months earlier also contributes to his current state of disorientation and his preoccupation with death, and no doubt causes him to contemplate his own death.[6] Although Will was somewhat less than perfectly matched with Marion, he took great pleasure in assisting her, running errands for her, and helping her to maneuver her heavy body out of cars. As long as his wife lived, Will could fulfill his old need to be "of use." And whatever the weaknesses of their marriage, Will's life with Marion did allow him to forget about his father. In one of the "dialogues" with his dead father, Will describes his "little Yankee life":

> So I went away, as far as I could get from you, knowing only that if I could turn 180 degrees away from you and your death-dealing there would be something different out there, different from death, maybe even a kind of life. And there was.
>
> I went as far as I could go, married a rich hardheaded plain decent crippled pious upstate Utica, New York, woman, practiced Trusts and Estates law in a paneled office on Wall Street. . . . Now Marion is dead and I can't believe I spent all those years in New York in Trusts and Estates and taking dogs down elevators and out to the park to take a crap (72–73).

With Marion gone, Will begins to think about his father after keeping him out of his consciousness for 20 years: "Now he remembered everything his father said and did, even remembered the smell of him, the catarrh-and-whiskey breath and the hot, quail reek of his hands" (71). Will may also be preoccupied with death because he has reached the age that his father was when he shot himself in the attic of their house. As he now remembers and deals with his father, whom he addresses throughout the novel as "old mole," Hamlet's epithet for his father's ghost, Will is at that stage in life when Marcel suggests that the perception of one's life alters: "In spite of everything that is implied by the current belief that time's arrow flies only one way, a man, as he grows older, has nearly always the feeling that he is growing nearer to his childhood; though the gap of years between him and his childhood is growing, at the same time, wider and wider" (*MB* 1: 240).

Throughout the novel, Will remembers a hunting trip that he took with his father in Georgia when he was 12 years old. For the disoriented Will Barrett, what occurred during this hunting trip becomes the *only* event that has ever happened to him: "Everything else that had happened afterwards was a non-event" (52). In the light of Will's obsession with the hunting trip, Marcel's observation that "the contamination of the future by the past is one of the sources of fatalism" seems particularly pertinent (*CF* 52). Will's memory of the hunting trip "contaminates" his present life and abnegates the possibility of his having a future unless he can lay the ghost of his father to rest once and for all. Will is certain that his father was trying to tell him something: "He was trying to tell me that one day I would come to the same place he came to, and I have" (62). Because of his own advancing age, Will is haunted by his father's claim "You and I are the same" (55). Such an assertion of likeness may mean that he is doomed to repeat his father's suicide.

Will finally pieces together the events of that childhood hunting trip: his father tried to shoot him with both barrels of the 12-gauge Greener and then reloaded and turned the shotgun on himself. It is no wonder that nearly 40 years after the event, Will continually falls to the ground.[7] In the present of the novel, Will Barrett stands on a golf course in North Carolina and remembers being hit by gunshot: "[The boy] found himself down in the leaves without knowing how he got there . . . when he tried to stand, the keening in his ear spun him down again. . . . It was as if someone had taken hold of him and flung him down" (56). Later he determines that since his father could hit a quail at 50 feet and yet had nearly missed him at 15 feet, his father must have pulled up in the last split second before firing. But "Was it love or failure of love" (148) that made his father hesitate, resulting in a shot that grazed Will's cheek?

Will's father's action, turning the shotgun on young Will, is the supreme betrayal of fatherhood, diametrically opposed, according to Marcel, to how a person who loves another acts: "To love a being . . . is to say you, you in particular, will never die. . . . To consent to the death of a being is in a sense to give him up to death" (*HV* 147). Will's father has, therefore, twice betrayed his son, first by "giving him up to death" by turning the Greener on him, and then a few years later by committing suicide. Will's father has left him a terrible legacy; he has passed on to his son his fear of life, his fascination with death, and his burden of self-loathing. Will also suffers from the guilt of the survivor; knowing that his father meant to kill him combined with the betrayal of his father's desertion by suicide deals Will a double blow. It is astonishing that he has lived as well as he has. Reflecting on the hunting trip, Will says:

> He killed me then and I did now know it. I even thought he had missèd me. I have been living, yes, but it is a living death because I knew he wanted me dead. Am I entitled to live? I am alive by a fluke like the sole survivor of Treblinka, who lived by a fluke, but did not really feel entitled to live (324).

It also seems likely that Will's fascination with Armageddon can be laid at his father's door. Will exists in a state of anxiety that makes him more comfortable being shot at than not being shot at. Returning home from a golf game, Will Barrett hears shots ring out and takes refuge under the Rolls Royce in his five-car garage, as if Ewell McBee's stray shots signal the beginning of the Battle of Armageddon for which Will secretly yearns. "I know why it is better to be shot at on a Sunday afternoon than not be shot at," Will muses, "Because it means maybe there *is* an enemy after all" (21). Although he is not a believer, Will has developed "ideas of reference" and is caught up in eschatological speculation, convinced that all the Jews are leaving North Carolina to return to the Holy Land, a sure sign of the Second Coming (11). J. Gerald Kennedy concentrates on the ambiguity that arises from reading signs. Kennedy suggests that Will Barrett confronts a dilemma: "whether the observed signs of the Last Days comprise a coded, divine inscription or a self-generated delusion, a symptom of alienation and madness."[8] Because he is reluctant to repeat his father's suicide,

Will longs for an end to his life for which he cannot be held responsible. If the Last Days are at hand, Will will know what to do and will not have to face the problem of living. He is like Percy's man who is more worried that the bomb will not fall than that it will; the problem of what to do if the bomb does *not* fall involves facing the ordinary mystery of living from day to day in a world where a man cannot face four o'clock in the afternoon.[9]

Will tries to draw his old friend Sutter Vaught into his delusion, urging him to "establish an observation post in the village of Megiddo" from which Sutter can "monitor any unusual events in the Arab countries to the east, particularly the emergence of a leader of extraordinary abilities—another putative sign of the last days" (194). Later, in Lost Cove cave, Will decides that if a sign comes from God that the Last Days are at hand, "I shall go to Megiddo with Sutter and wait for the Stranger from the East" (212–13). Watching and waiting for the Antichrist would be considerably easier for Will Barrett than dealing with his own pain and sorrow.[10]

As William Rodney Allen has shown, Will's obsession with the Last Days may be seen as a reflection of his father's death wish raised to a general level.[11] Even the language Will uses to describe his father's despair echoes Scripture. In one of his "conversations" with his father, Will says: "Ever since your death, all I ever wanted from you was out. . . . out from the ancient hatred and allegiances, allegiances unto death and love of war and rumors of war and under it all death and your secret love of death" (72). We are reminded of Jesus's warning to his disciples that the end of the age would be marked by many false prophets and that they would hear of "wars and rumors of wars" (Matthew 24: 6). Will's eschatological yearnings are connected to his memories of the hunting trip. When his father tried to kill him, he established a pattern of Father as destroyer, one who is the author of one's life *and* of one's death. Thus Will identifies the warlike God of the Last Days with his father. If the Last Days are at hand, Will Barrett's death will be God's fault and not his own. Filled with these speculations about the end of the world, Will Barrett descends into Lost Cove cave to put God to a test.

With hubris aforethought, Will decides not to waste his death as he believes his father did but to use the risk of his death to answer one of the biggest questions of all—whether or not God exists. The half-mad Will declares, "My suicide will represent progress in the history of suicide. Unlike my father's it will be done in good faith, logically, neatly, and unobtrusively" (211). In a letter to Sutter, who is now living a life of relative calm in Albuquerque, Will explains that he will force the hidden God to make a move:

> My death, if it occurs, shall occur not by my own hand but by the hand of God. Or rather the handlessness or inaction of God.
>
> If I die, it will not be by my own hand but through the dereliction of another. It is not my intention to die but to live. Therefore, should I die, it will not be suicide. . . . I aim to settle the question of God once and for all (186).

And after he has explained his plan, in veiled language so that Sutter will not try to prevent the experiment, he triumphantly asks, "Can you discover a single flaw in this logic?" and declares, "I've got him! No more tricks! No more *deus absconditus*!" (192). Will's reference to the hidden God shows that he is close to the despair that doomed his father. As Marcel writes, "What is the meaning of despair if not a declaration that God has withdrawn himself from me?" (*HV* 47).

The problem with Will's updated version of Pascal's wager is that he attempts to force grace, assuming that, like Jacob, he can wrestle with God until God gives in. It never occurs to the mad Will Barrett that he and God are ontologically *other* and that God's grace cannot be demanded, that God's action or inaction will prove nothing. When Will descends into Lost Cove cave, he leaves the world of the living and joins his father underground, shut off from light and others. He is as blind as the minnows in the cave pools, as blind as his father, the old mole. He even imagines his father's approval of his action. When he hears their old servant D'Lo's voice asking, "What are you doing down here in the cold cold ground, massa?", Will asks his father, "What am I doing down here under the earth with you, old mole?" To which he imagines his father responds, "There is no other place for you" (215).

Although Will thinks that he has foreseen every possible occurrence, providing himself with enough Placidyl tablets to make his wait easier, something unexpected happens. He develops a terrible toothache which produces nausea and drives all secondary concerns, such as the existence of God, completely out of his head:

> There is one sure cure for cosmic explorations, grandiose ideas about God, man, death, suicide, and such—and that is nausea. I defy a man afflicted with nausea to give a single thought to these vast subjects. A nauseated man is a sober man. A nauseated man is a disinterested man.
> What does a nauseated person care about the Last Days? (213).

The gnawing persistence of an abscessed tooth draws all attention to itself and returns Will to his body, reminding him none too gently that he is, after all, not a spiritual being who can hold discourse with God but an *incarnated* being. As is so often the case in Percy's novels, physical ordeal causes Will Barrett to experience what Marcel calls "the sort of irresistible encroachment of my body upon me which is at the basis of my state as man or creature" (*BH* 83). Although an abscessed tooth is certainly not the sign that Will had in mind, it may in fact *be* a sign.[12] Instead of God's appearing or sending word as he had hoped, Will suffers pain that recalls him to what Marcel calls the basic "given" of metaphysics—incarnation.[13] Delirious with pain and nausea, he abandons his watch, wanders through the cave looking for a way out and eventually falls out of the cave and into Allison Huger's greenhouse. In Allie, the schizophrenic daughter of his old flame, Kitty Vaught, he discovers the "other" with whom he can inhabit the world.

From the time that Will first encounters Allie, having followed the balls that he has sliced "out of bounds" on the golf course, their potential importance to each other is suggested. Just as Binx saw Kate as "I myself" and Will Barrett once saw himself in Kitty Vaught, Will recognizes Allie: "Where had he seen her before? For one odd moment she was as familiar to him as he himself" (77). In fact, Will has good reason to think that Allie is familiar since she is Kitty's daughter and resembles both her mother and, apparently, her Uncle Sutter, for Will later tells her, "You're Sutter turned happy" (263).

But perhaps the most important resemblance is to his own younger self. When Will meets Allie Huger, he is given another chance at finding an intersubjective relationship based on an intuitive knowledge of likeness. Like Will in *The Last Gentleman*, Allie has problems with amnesia; she has difficulty remembering her own name. Like the younger Will, she has problems with living an "ordinary" life. Allie remembers her father's disappointment when she returned home after failing in the world: "Now he remembers I didn't finish school, I didn't get a job, I didn't get married, I didn't get engaged, I didn't even go steady. I didn't move on like I was supposed to. I made straight A's and flunked ordinary living" (93). Allie is *like* Will. She is Will's "thou," who is most purely "another I," the "I" that one can love incarnated in another being. Allie is another subject who makes his own subjectivity available to him.

In this novel for the first time, Percy devotes all his considerable talents to developing a believable and moving intersubjective relationship. For the first seven chapters, he alternates between Will Barrett and Allison Huger as point-of-view characters. Percy gives Allison far more time than he has devoted to any other female character.[14] In an interview, he remarks that he purposely loaded the initial meeting of Will and Allie with symbolic significance:

> [Will is] overwhelmed by the past and, at the same time, he slices out of bounds . . . and there is sunlight shining on this girl. So he has the confluence of three things at once at one point: the old life, the life of despair; his present life, which is going nowhere, falling down; now all of a sudden, a literal ray of hope. The sunlight actually breaks through the pine trees and he sees the girl, whom he *thinks* is a boy. Well, it's kind of grace in a way; after all, you don't plan on grace.[15]

The hope which Allie represents for Will is also suggested in another way, through Percy's use of Marcellian language. At the end of his first meeting with Allie, as Will walks away from the greenhouse, his total recall is described: "He remembered everything, even the joke which Jimmy had told him twenty years before. He even remembered the future" (79). What is most interesting here is the sentence, "He even remembered the future," because the language is so close to one of Marcel's definitions of hope:

> Despair is in a certain sense the consciousness of time as closed or, more exactly still, of time as a prison—whilst hope appears as piercing through time; everything happens as though time, instead

of hedging consciousness round, allowed something to pass through it. . . . Of course one cannot say that hope sees what is going to happen; but it affirms as *if* it saw. . . . hope aims at reunion, at recollection, at reconciliation: in that way, and in that way alone, it might be called a *memory of the future* (*HV* 53. Italics added).

The novel, then, becomes the story of Will Barrett's choice between despair and hope, death and life, the past and the future—represented by his dead father and Allie Huger, respectively.

When Allie is introduced in the second chapter, she has just escaped from the Valleyhead Sanitarium where she has been a patient since her mother found her curled up in a closet, completely withdrawn from the world, about two years ago. At Valleyhead, Allie was subjected to electroshock therapy which has left her with almost no memory. Before leaving the mental hospital, Allie explained to Dr. Duk that she needed to go deep inside in order to find herself: "I have to go down down before I go up. Down down in me to it. You shouldn't try to keep me up by buzzing me up" (90). Dr. Duk's shock treatments only serve to abstract Allie further from herself. Allie plans to avoid future shock treatments: "*No buzzin cousin*" and "*Fried is crucified*" says Allie's own voice during the interview that her parents have with Dr. Duk to discuss her future, but it sounds more like a radio to her (90).

Apparently the shock treatments have the effect of temporarily raising Allie's spirits; she is not so withdrawn after treatment, but she is also not herself. But like Tom More's lapsometer, the treatments provide only temporary improvement. They are no better than drugs taken to return the self to itself. Allie remembers previous experiments with drugs: "Drugs: not bad. In my bed in Front Street apartment or in closet, getting out of it with yellowjacks and going down down toward *it*, Sirius or black hole, but not really, only seeming to, because when you come out of it you're nowhere, not an inch closer to Sirius" (94–95). "Buzzing" artificially raises Allie, whereas drugs simulate the movement down to the self within. Both means are artificial, and neither has staying power.

Although Allie's sinking into herself might be seen as a rejection of others, it in fact demonstrates Marcel's concept of "fidelity to oneself" which prepares the ground for a real encounter with the "other":

> Fidelity to oneself is both difficult to achieve and to discern. In order to be faithful to oneself it is first of all necessary to remain alive, and that is precisely what it is not easy to do. . . . the more I am able to preserve this intimacy with myself, the more I shall be capable of making real contact with my neighbor, and by neighbor I do not mean one of those depersonalized others whose jeers and censures I fear, but the particular human being I met at a definite time in my life who . . . has come for good into the personal universe which, as it were, wraps me round (*HV* 131).

As Allie recovers from her most recent electroshock treatment, she is initially happy in her new self as audience to her old self; she reads entries from her notebook, INSTRUCTIONS FROM MYSELF TO MYSELF. Having written these entries before the most recent shock treatment, she now uses them as a road map for organizing her life in the greenhouse.[16] For a period of time, Allie contains within herself an "I," the old self who wrote the notes, and a "thou," the post-shock-treatment self who can barely remember her own name without looking it up on her driver's license: "She uttered her name aloud. At first it sounded strange. Then she recognized it as her name" (24).[17] The "I" who is writing is clearly distinguished from the "you" who will later read the Instructions:

> I, that is you, but for the present as I write this, I—am scheduled to be buzzed early Wednesday morning. . . . I am writing this in my room in the closed wing (you may not remember the room when you read this on October 22, but it will come back), from which there is no escape, else I'd be long gone (27).

Like Kate Cutrer, Allie has discovered her own freedom—"What was my (your, our) discovery? That I could *act*. I was *free* to act" (40). By writing instructions in her notebook, Allie uses her relatively stable, pre-shock therapy self to organize a new life for the self that she knows will be completely at a loss after the shock treatment. The "I" who speaks shows love and compassion for the "you" who will be disoriented. Instead of relying upon her parents and her therapist, Dr. Duk, who have betrayed her, Allie takes charge of her own life, functions as her own parent, offering encouragement and reassurance: "Take a hot bath. Eat and sleep for twenty-four hours. You'll be very hungry after the buzz (remember?) and tired and sore. You'll feel like a rape victim in every way but one" (29). The voice of a self-created mother gives simple advice: go to bed, rest, eat, sleep. Having been betrayed by others, Allie cannot reach out to the "other" until she learns to trust herself. Allie demonstrates the healthy kind of self-love which Marcel argues will make her available to others. Marcel carefully distinguishes between an "idolatrous" love of self and a "charity towards oneself" which is necessary if the ego is to grow. Charity towards oneself nourishes the self and "considers it as a seed which must be cultivated, as a ground which must be readied for the spiritual or even the divine in this world. To love oneself in this second sense is not the same as self-complacency, but is rather an attitude towards the self which permits its maximum development" (*CF* 46).

Allison Huger is another of Percy's sovereign wayfarers, Marcel's *homo viator*, who starts life anew. While she is still in the hospital, Allie understands her sovereignty, "What if *I* make the plans for me? What then? Is there an I in me that can start something? An initiating I, an I-I" (105). Percy even places her in a greenhouse to emphasize the metaphor of a woman in the garden where she can make a clearing for being, first her own and then Will's.

Unlike her mother, Allie is no consumer of prepared experience. Because the shock treatments have wiped out much of her memory, she has few preconceptions. She hardly knows how to speak her own native language. Like a child, Allie misses idiomatic meanings and metaphors: "She took words seriously to mean more or less what they said, but other people seemed to use words as signals in another code they had agreed upon" (34). For example, Allie can make no sense of bumper stickers because she doesn't understand their context. She cannot figure out the referent of the pronoun "it" on two bumper stickers she sees: "DO IT IN A PICKUP" and "I FOUND IT" (22), the first depending upon the hearer understanding the linguistic context, a chain of other such sayings and referring to sex, the second taking up the allusion and substituting Christ, or being "born again," for the ultimate experience. Allie needs words in order to live a life, and when Will Barrett gives her the name of the object that she needs in order to move the stove, a "creeper," she treats the word as a gift: "He noticed that she treated the gift of the word exactly like the avocados. She'd have to think about it after he left" (115).

Her determination to move the old cast-iron Grand Crown stove by herself is an example of Allie's desire to assert her sovereignty. She could ask Will Barrett to help, but to ask, to expect something from him would be to be beholden to him: "No, she hadn't asked him because she didn't want to ask anybody. Asking is losing, she might have said. Or getting help is behelt. It is not that a debt is incurred to a person for a thing as that the thing itself loses value. It was her stove and her life and she would move the stove and live her life" (92). Allie's first approach to her new life must be to gain control over the objects that are in her world, the largest and most imposing of which is the old stove. This way, according to Percy, lies sanity. In a remembered conversation with Dr. Duk, Allie expresses the comfort to be found in ordinary objects: "To stay sane, learn about wrens, mums, Orion" (90). At first Allie lives happily with a set of problems to be solved, making lists of what she will need to buy, consulting the local library for the names that she needs—a block and tackle pulley, for example, to move the stove.

So long as life can be seen as a series of problems to be confronted, Allie can think of what to do. When Will Barrett falls into her greenhouse, he at first presents her only with another problem. Here and elsewhere in the novel, Percy employs Marcel's categories of problem and mystery to point out the differences between Allie's original approach to Will and her eventual understanding of him as a person to be encountered.[18] Allie is comfortable dealing with the unconscious Will because he is like the stove: "When he landed on the floor of her greenhouse, knocking himself out, he was a problem to be solved, like moving the stove. Problems are for solving. Alone" (233). Employing a combination of tools—a "single double-gain pulley," a creeper and a rope sling—Allie hoists Will onto a bed (235). Perfectly comfortable with this unconscious man, whose ontological state is that of an object, Allie tends to his needs, washes his body and his clothes.

Because Will does not look at her, Allie can appreciate him:

"How nice people are, unconscious! They do not glance" (235). Allie has a Sartrean understanding of the danger of the glance. She has had all she wants of people's eyes boring into her and threatening her very self. Other people's looks are an "impalement and a derailment" to Allie (233). She is comfortable only with her dog because when she looks directly at him, he averts his eyes. But people look directly at her.

When Will regains consciousness, he becomes something more than a problem: "It was no trouble handling him until he came to and looked at her, She could do anything if nobody watched her." (233). Interestingly, however, Allie does not object to this particular man's looking at her: "The man watched her from the bunk but she didn't mind. His look was not controlling or impaling but soft and gray and going away. Her back felt his and the dog's eyes following her, but when she faced them, their eyes rolled up into their eyebrows" (242). Since Will is far from well himself, he does not frighten Allie.

We have been prepared for Allie's eventual recognition of Will Barrett as the "other" before he falls from the cave into her greenhouse. Upon her second encounter with Will, when he brings her gifts of avocados and canned meat, Allie wants to ask him who he is: "For a moment she wondered if she had considered saying something crazy like "Are you my lover?" Or "Are you my father?" (109). Although she does not voice these questions, she does notice that she feels free to talk to this distracted man because of "a certain tentativeness in him that waited on her, like the dog, even now and then cocking an eye in her direction" (110).

After Will regains consciousness, Allie almost immediately realizes that she will do anything he asks her. Will obligingly gives her a series of errands to perform for him, and Allie revels in her discovery of "what people in the world do" (246). She thinks she has come upon the great secret of life: "She had thought (and her mother had expected) that she must do something extraordinary, be somebody extraordinary. Whereas the trick lay in leading the most ordinary life imaginable, get an ordinary job, in itself a joy in its very ordinariness, and *then* be as extraordinary or ordinary as one pleased" (247). The first indication that Allie's feelings for Will are deepening into love is seen when she undertakes one of his errands, asking Dr. Vance Battle to come and see him. Allie has difficulty giving Will's name to Dr. Battle because somehow his name is not enough to name him: "What to call *him*? Mr. Barrett? Mr. Will? Will Barrett? Bill Barrett? Williston Bibb Barrett? None of the names fit. A name would give him form once and for all. He would flow into its syllables and junctures and there take shape forever. She didn't want him named" (249). The Marcellian undertones in Allie's reluctance to name Will are unmistakable. Marcel observes that one cannot really name the beloved "other" in such a way as to encompass his or her being: "Whoever has loved knows that what he loved in the other cannot be reduced to discernible qualities—and in exactly the same way the mystery of what I am in myself is the very thing about me which is only revealed to love" (*HV* 132). Percy builds on Marcel's idea, observing that the self is basically unformulable to itself, that human beings, who name everything else in the universe, cannot successfully name themselves. In "Naming and Being," Percy writes: "Everything else in the world tends to become ever more densely formulated by its name: *this* is a chair, *that* is a ball, *you* are Robert. . . . But I myself escape every such attempt at formulation. . . . This is not to say that I am nothing: this is only to say that I am that which I cannot name."[19]

Allie's problem comes from the fact that heretofore words have been devices for naming objects for her. They were useful so long as they allowed her to ask for items in a hardware store, but Will Barrett is a person whom she is beginning to love. She does not want him encapsulated and impaled by his name. When he was a problem to her, perhaps his name would have been sufficient. Objects can be named; people are presences who have names, but their names do not function in the same way. Percy notes that the "thou" is no more pinned down by a name than "I" am: "Nor are you formulable under the auspices of a symbol. If I do conceive you as a something in the world rather than as a co-celebrant of the world, I fall from the I-thou to the I-It."[20]

Confronted with the mystery of love, Allie uses the exact method that worked successfully for her when she needed information about pulleys; she goes to the library to look it up. But "Love" is not a problem accessible to this empirical approach. After finding a number of sentences which have love as their subject such as "Love begets love," "Love conquers all things," "Love is truth and truth is beauty," "Love is blind," and "Love is love's reward," Allie responds, "Oh my God. . . . What does all that *mean?* These people are crazier than I am" (240–41). As long as Allie's life was a series of problems to be solved—buying tools, moving the stove— Allie could keep herself company, be both "I" and "thou," but the mystery of love requires an "other." In the long run, Allie's newfound freedom depends upon finding another person whom she can address as "thou" because, as Marcel reminds us, "my freedom cannot fully affirm itself unless it embraces my personal destiny and does not claim merely to survey it. . . . this destiny is not deepened or enriched unless it is open to others" (*CF* 31).

When Will interrupts their initial lovemaking to tell her about himself, Allie is so caught up in his words that she cannot follow what he says:

> When he began to talk she found that she could not hear his words for listening to the way he said them. Was he saying the words for the words themselves, for what they meant, or for what they could do to her? There was something about the way he talked that reminded her of her own rehearsed sentences. . . . Though he hardly touched her, his words seemed to flow across all parts of her body. Were they meant to? A pleasure she had never known before bloomed deep in her body. Was this a way of making love? (262)

Here the pleasure Allie takes in Will's words is likened to the pleasure of orgasm. Long before they make love, Will and Allie experience privileged moments of communication that ground their developing love soundly in a shared consciousness. Will's ability to fathom Allie's meaning (we remember his uncanny "radar" in *The Last Gentleman*) suggests that their intersubjective conversations are inextricably part of their love for each other. When they speak, each becomes spiritually available to the other. In Allie's strange way of talking—ordinary words hooked together in extra-ordinary ways—Will hears both "other voices in other years" and "another voice, something new and not quite formed" (109). Will's taking the time to talk with Allie, to attempt to tell her who he is and to get to know her, bodes well for their eventual relationship.

He does not make love to her in the greenhouse even though Allie is more than willing and asks him: "I said why did you stop. I mean I meant to say 'it.' Why did you stop? I think this is 'it'" (258). But Will moves slowly with Allie, who is rapidly becoming very precious to him. He knows that he has to leave the greenhouse and straighten out the problems he has set in motion by his cave experiment, and he wants to give his relationship with Allie every chance.

Like Binx Bolling and Tom More, Will now resolves to participate in his own life, to take care of those who need him. As he leaves the greenhouse, Will tells Allie that he is going to do "What is expected of me. Take care of people who need taking care of. I have to see how my daughter is. . . . I have not been a good father" (265). And he assures Allie that she is one of the people he will take care of. But before he can commit himself to Allie, he must come face to face with his father's legacy of death.

His cave wounds mostly healed but with his pH still unusually high, Will Barrett makes his way to his Mercedes, which Allie has left in the parking lot of the Linwood Country Club. After suffering another flashback to a trip he took out west with his father when he was 13, Will experiences a breakthrough. Alone in the parking lot, he dances around like an insane person, chanting what the narrator calls a "peculiar litany": "I know your name at last, he said, laughing and hooting *hee hee hooooee* like a pig-caller and kicking the tires, and you are not going to prevail over me" (272). Will Barrett dances like Tom More on Christmas Eve to celebrate the sovereignty that he claims over death by naming it:

> Death in the guise of love shall not prevail over me. . . . Death in the guise of Christianity is not going to prevail over me. . . . Death in the guise of belief is not going to prevail over me. . . . Death in the guise of isms and asms shall not prevail over me, orgasm, enthusiasm, liberalism, conservatism, Communism, Buddhism, Americanism, for an ism is only another way of despairing of the truth (272–73).

Being able to name death gives Will power over the attraction that death holds for him. Will accuses his father of giving in to death and then exclaims: "To know the many names of death is also to know there is life. I choose life" (274). Naming even grants power over the "death genes" that Will fears he may have inherited from his father: "Death in the form of death genes shall not prevail over me, for death genes are one thing but it is something else to name the death genes and know them and stand over against them and dare them. I am different from my death genes and therefore not subject to them" (274). This centrally important passage illustrates Percy's assertion that naming can lead to control over the object. By naming all the manifestations of death, Will Barrett asserts his freedom and control over his own death wish and chooses life.

The "litany" section is followed by a kind of vision which Will experiences, apparently because his pH is out of balance. Exhausted after his frenzied dismissal of death, Will sinks into a deep sleep and has "a swift sure presentiment of what lay in store" (204). In the dream, Will sees the same patch of ground where once there stood a springhouse when he was a boy become progressively a part of a golf course, a subdivision, a shopping center, and finally a deserted shopping center. Will sees himself in the ruined shopping center:

> When he came to years from now, he was lying on the spot. The skylight of the mall was broken. The terrazo was cracked. . . . A raccoon lived in the Orange Julius stand. No one was there. Yet something moved and someone spoke. . . . Very well, since you've insisted on it, here it is, the green-stick Rosebud gold-bug matador, the great distinguished thing (277).

Will Barrett's dream is clearly of his own death. In a masterful sentence that contains allusions to four writers and a classic film, Percy gives Will what he has been searching for—some of the "many names of death." The unidentified voice tells Will that he will now come face to face with "the green stick Rosebud gold-bug matador, the great distinguished thing." The first three words, *green-stick*, *rosebud* and *gold-bug*, are nouns functioning as adjectives, and they allude to Tolstoy, *Citizen Kane* and Poe. They modify the noun, *matador*, Hemingway's embodiment of grace in the face of death.[21] In apposition to the noun *matador*, we have a phrase attributed to Henry James. Leon Edel reports that Edith Wharton said that James had told a mutual friend that when he suffered a stroke on 2 December 1915, his first thought was "So it has come at last—the Distinguished Thing."[22]

Will's final choice of life over death is delayed briefly, however, while he is hospitalized at St. Mark's Convalescent Home so that his pH can be monitored every few hours and he can be given the hydrogen ion that he lacks. Although Will tolerates the ion treatment well, he loses control of his life. He finally leaves the convalescent center because, although "he seemed in a queer way to prosper," his life is out of his hands. And even though the treatment causes him to forget his delusion that the Jews are leaving North Carolina, he does not forget Allie: "He wanted to see Allie. He forgot about Jews but not Allie. Had his longing for her been a hydrogen-ion deficiency, a *wahnsinnige Sehnsucht*? No, hydrogen or no hydrogen, he wanted to see her face" (307). But even after Will has remembered Allie and removed her to a Holiday Inn where she will be safe from her mother and Dr. Duk, he wakes and has one final "dialogue" with his father, who calls to Will to come to him, to find the guns: "Come, it's the only way, the one quick sure exit of grace and violence and beauty. Come, believe me, it's the ultimate come" (336–37). The father's voice is eloquent in its final appeal, reminding Will of the horrors that may accompany old age: "Very well, let it close you out with the drools and the shakes and your mouth fallen open, head nodding away and both hands rolling pills. But you'll never even get that far because you've got my genes and you know better" (337).

Instead of heeding his father and blowing his brains out, however, Will asserts his independence. He rises, retrieves the leather gun case from the car and walks off into the night: "When he reached the overlook the Holiday Inn looked over, he did not even pause but swung the case like a discus, the throw turning him around and heading him back. He did not hear the Greener hit bottom. As an afterthought, he pitched the Luger back over his shoulder and went away without listening" (338). By taking this action, Will demonstrates both the sovereignty that he claimed over death when he named it and his hope for a new life. As Marcel says, hope is the act by which the temptation to despair is overcome (*HV* 36). Hope is not a "kind of listless waiting," according to Marcel, but rather an active force that is closely related to the will: "[Hope] underpins action or it runs before it. . . . Hope seems to me the prolongation into the unknown of an activity which is central—that is to say, rooted in being. Hence it has affinities, not with desire, but with the will. . . . Could not hope therefore be defined as the will when it is made to bear on what does not depend on itself?" (*PE* 33). Thus when Will throws the weapons away, he takes the step that leads ultimately to his declaration that he will have both Allie and God. With Allie and the hope that she embodies in his life, Will has found the strength to say No in thunder to his father, and he is released to live in the present with Allie. Only after he has disposed of the weapons do he and Allie consummate their love.

The ontological closeness which makes their sexual loving the logical next development is expressed in language that echoes a passage in *The Last Gentleman*: "There was an angle but it did not make trouble. Entering her was like turning a corner and coming home" (339). This stands in direct opposition to the failed love-making between Kitty and Will where "the angles were bad and contrived against him" (*LG* 252). In Allie and Will's case, success on the existential level leads to success on the sexual level, just as failure on the existential level doomed Kitty and Will's sexual attempt. After Allie and Will have made love, they remain in the body, incarnated:

> Each tended to the other, kneading and poking sore places. She examined him like a mother examining a child, close, stretching skin, her mouth open, grabbing hair to pull his head over to see his neck, her eyes slightly abulge with concentration, checking his cave wounds, picking at scabs. When her eyes happened to meet his, they softened and went deep. Eyes examining are different from eyes meeting eyes. . . . Then she smiled and flew against him again (341–42).

This is the first time in all of Percy's novels where eyes meet and "go deep," the look of love passing from an "I" to a "thou" and back again. Allie and Will look lovingly into each other's eyes and affirm an intersubjectivity free from fear.

Even with his pH level soaring, Will manages to plan a new life with Allie—a life that will include marriage and children. It is no longer necessary for either of them to retreat from the world. When Allie suggests to Will that they can hide from her mother and Dr. Duk in the cave, Will tells her, "We don't have to go in the cave.

The cave is over and done with. We can live up here now" (331). Will plans to work as a lawyer, clerking for Mr. Slocum until he passes the bar exam. Allie will work in her greenhouse with the help of Mr. Eberhart and her old friend Kelso from Valleyhead Sanatarium. The rudiments of a community organized around meaningful work are all here, as Will plans the division of Allie's land into ten-acre parcels upon which the old men whom Will has met at St. Mark's Convalescent Home will build log cabins. The love which Will and Allie share now reaches out to include others who have been institutionalized so that they too may again live as free people and control their own lives.

And finally God Himself, Marcel's absolute Thou, the hidden God whom Will sought in the cave, is available to Will. Observing the tender care that two orderlies demonstrate for an old woman, Will wonders, "Does goodness come tricked out so as fakery and fondness and carrying on and is God himself as sly? (349). Like Walker Percy, Will Barrett refuses to accept anything less than "the infinite mystery and the infinite delight, i.e., God."[23] Will has not lost his knack for "discerning people" and knowing when they know something he does not. He senses that Father Weatherbee, the old Episcopal priest who believes in the Apostolic Succession, is a man of authority who can tell him what he needs to know. Having committed himself to Allie, Will goes to Father Weatherbee and confronts him in a triumphant final passage:

> Will Barrett stopped the old priest at the door and gazed into his face. The bad eye spun and the good eye looked back at him fearfully: What do you want of me? What do I want of him, mused Will Barrett, and suddenly realized he had gripped the old man's wrists as if he were a child. . . . Will Barrett thought about Allie in her greenhouse, her wide gray eyes, her lean muscled boy's arms, her strong quick hands. His heart leapt with a secret joy. What is it I want from her and him, he wondered, not only want but must have? Is she a gift and therefore a sign of a giver? Could it be that the Lord is here, masquerading behind this simple holy face? Am I crazy to want both, her and Him? No, not want, must have. And will have (360).

Although the language Will uses is that of willing himself to have God, what is here named *will* is consonant with Marcel's *hope*, since the will cannot operate in the realm of the transcendent. Once a quality like will is made to bear on the transcendent, it is transformed into hope. This radiant hope, embodied in Allie, effectively counteracts Will's dead father's despair.

In an interview, Percy describes Will Barrett at the end of the novel: "He wants the best of both worlds; he wants Allie and he wants Jesus Christ."[24] Will demands both the immanent and the transcendent: Allie is an immanent being through whose love Will catches sight of transcendent love, the love of God. Allie is the sign that Will demanded from God when he went into Lost Cove cave. According to Marcel, even the transcendent must somehow be available to experience: "The urgent inner need for transcendence should never be interpreted as a need to pass beyond all experience whatsoever; for beyond all experience, there is nothing; I do not say merely nothing that can be thought, but nothing that can be felt" (*MB* 1: 59). Marcel here links the transcendent realm to the immanent, asserting that something that is not in some way connected to an individual's way of being as an incarnated creature cannot be thought of. William Rodney Allen observes that Allie "seems too firmly rooted to the earth to be much concerned with heaven" and that therefore she may not be able to join Will in his quest for transcendent meaning.[25] But it seems that Allie's connection with the immanent is exactly what Will Barrett needs to prevent him from falling prey to abstraction. Percy suggests that God's presence is made manifest in the most *ordinary* of human experiences, in human love and in an openness to the wonders of the physical world. Certainly Will Barrett believes that the intersubjective love he shares with Allie is a sign of transcendent love.

The action, then, that begins with Will's discarding the weapons culminates in his declaration that he will have it all, an exultant affirmation of life and love. Will's quests have become one in this final passage. Will Barrett *wills* to have it all, Allie and marriage, the human intersubjective relationship, a community of people, and Father Weatherbee's God, the One who has given him Allie to love.

"The Thanatos Syndrome"

Abstraction Ascendant

Percy's critics have observed how well *The Second Coming* ties together his major concerns. William Rodney Allen, for example, suggests that *The Second Coming* provides "a sense of closure . . . a feeling of the rounding off of an imaginative world" because in this novel Percy finally finds novelistic expression for the nightmare of a father's suicide.[1] Jac Tharpe notes that *The Second Coming* "quite as neatly rounds out a career as if it had been designed for that purpose."[2] I have argued that *The Second Coming* illustrates how Will Barrett's recognition of Allie Huger as a gift from God makes possible an intersubjective relationship that is both secular and religious. But Percy is not content to stop with the triumph of eros over thanatos achieved in *The Second Coming*. In his sixth novel, *The Thanatos Syndrome*, Percy returns to Tom More, the alcoholic physician of *Love in the Ruins* and to the public world of Feliciana Parish. All is not well in Fedville.

Instead of the Second Coming that Tom More was half anticipating at the end of *Love in the Ruins*, what this world has produced is more of the same—more great vaulting abstract systems that threaten subjectivity. The Qualitarians whom More opposed in the Pit have come into power under the leadership of Bob Comeaux, whose prime consideration is engineering a good life for all. Why should people need Armageddon when humankind is completely capable of engineering its own destruction—and from the best of motives—tenderness and caring? More's old friend Father Smith explains that all Satan had to do was to leave people to their own devices: "It is because God agreed to let the Great Prince Satan have his way with men for a hundred years—this one hundred years, the twentieth century. And he has. How did he do it? No great evil scenes, no demons—he's too smart for that. All he had to do was leave us alone. We did it. Reason warred with faith. Science triumphed. The upshot? One hundred million dead."[3] In *The Thanatos Syndrome*, Percy issues a warning that death is in the ascendancy in the 20th century, because the spirit of abstraction is abroad in the land.

The novel is set in 1995 or 1996, about seven years after the epilogue of *Love in the Ruins*.[4] Fresh from a two-year incarceration at Fort Pelham, Alabama, where he was sent for selling prescriptions to long-distance truckers, Tom More returns to discover that something is wrong with his patients. They have begun to display strange sexual behavior, and they speak in sentence fragments and willingly answer questions out of context. No longer devoted to the lapsometer to show just how short the self falls from itself, More has returned to the psychiatric faith he learned from Henry Stack Sullivan.[5] More believes what Sullivan taught him: "Each patient this side of psychosis, and even some psychotics, has the means of obtaining what he needs, she needs, with a little help from you" (16). More believes in the talking therapy and is at heart a modified Freudian, particularly when it comes to Freud's belief in the two main drives that man is prey to: Eros and Thanatos.

The Thanatos Syndrome, as John Edward Hardy observes, has two distinct plot lines.[6] The adventure story plot involves Tom More's successful routing of Bob Comeaux and his consortium of Fedville doctors who are secretly adding heavy sodium to the local water supply in order to engineer a new Eden where people will be better behaved and happier. The second plot concerns the developing intersubjective relationship between Dr. More and his old friend, Father Smith. Both plots reveal an intense scrutiny of language and its uses. In addition to the two plots, there are two planes of activity, one immanent and horizontal, the other transcendent and vertical. These two planes are dislocated, barely able to make contact. Father Smith, however, takes on importance as the one person who inhabits both realms. In the immanent world, he is a part-time fire watcher for the forestry service whose fire-spotting activity provides a paradigm for all intersubjective relationships. He determines one coordinate of a brushfire by using an ancient azimuth, but he must get another fix from a fire-spotter in the Waldheim tower in order to triangulate and locate the fire on his map. Father Smith embodies vertical movement when he climbs up into his fire tower out of the troubled world where the activities of the Fedville doctors remind him of the Weimar doctors whose interests in engineering a "pure race" provided a firm base for Hitler's maniacal anti-Semitism. He emerges from the background occupied by Percy's other distracted priests to center stage as the representative of the Church, who has advice and hope to offer Tom More. It is Father Smith alone who sees the real danger in Comeaux's social engineering, concluding that Comeaux's euthanasia program contributes mightily to the devaluation of human life. Smith's importance is further evidenced by Percy's efforts to steep the priest in some of his own experiences in Germany in 1934, biographical tidbits that Percy generally reserves for his protagonists.[7]

The first thing we notice about Father Smith is that he is utterly consistent with his earlier avatar, the befuddled, alcoholic priest of *Love in the Ruins* who occupies the bed next to More's in the Fedville Hospital acute ward. Certain that "Death is winning, life is losing," Father Smith was troubled in his vocation because he felt cut off from the transcendent: "the channels are jammed and the word is not getting through" (*LR* 184, 185). The priest, however, has undergone an interesting name change. In *Love in the Ruins* he is Father Rinaldo Smith; in the sequel he has become Father *Simon* Rinaldo Smith, and the new name signifies. His patron saint is, appropriately, St. Simeon Stylites, the first of the "pillar saints," a fifth century Syrian ascetic who made a life of sitting atop a series of increasingly higher platforms (the last approximately 60 feet high) to perform vicarious penance for the evil lives of his countrymen.

At times Father Smith nearly runs away with the novel because of the near nonpresence of Tom More, who is adrift in his own life, cut off from others, including the members of his own family. More's wife Ellen is away at a bridge tournament for most of the present action, and the care of young Meg and Tom is left to loyal family retainers. Even More's old friend, Max Gottlieb, whom he credits with twice saving his life in *Love in the Ruins*, is now associated with the enemy, Bob Comeaux. Although More has had intersubjective relationships with his patients, he has lost these important human connections because his patients are no longer anxious, no longer aware of themselves *as selves*.

Furthermore, More is remote from his own life. Far more passive and less morally outraged than he was in *Love in the Ruins*, More does not seem to be the principal actor in his own life. He claims to have achieved a clearer understanding of others during his time at Fort Pelham, and he has closely observed enough strange symptoms in his patients to believe that there is a "syndrome," but he is remarkably inept at making sense of his life despite the attempts of various friends to show him how he appears to them. For example, his housekeeper's daughter Chandra notes, "You too much up in your head. You don't even pay attention to folks when they talking to you. How you act in your office? Psychiatrists are supposed to be sensitive to the emotional needs of their patients, aren't they?" (40). Chandra's analysis of More's behavior is right on target, and her imitation of how he walks around with his eyes rolled back astute. But More, although he laughs at Chandra's impersonation, fails to take the comment to heart, getting caught up instead in Chandra's pronunciation ("ack" for "act")—in the form instead of the content.

More also refuses to make choices, a reluctance highlighted throughout the novel. He was relatively content to be incarcerated at Fort Pelham, and when he is arrested for the second time, he takes comfort in the "hard but comfortable" cot in his cell and muses: "There is something to be said for having no choice in what one does. I felt almost as good as I did in prison in Alabama" (262). All choices removed, More sleeps far better than he did the night before at Pantherburn. He is, though, vaguely aware of being responsible for what happens to him. When he first sees his cousin Lucy Lipscomb, epidemiologist and computer whiz, at Pantherburn, he knows what he is about to get himself into. Of Lucy, he remarks, "What a splendid, by no means small, woman. Again the smell of her cotton gives me a *déjà vu*. I know if I choose to know, but don't of course, what will happen next. And yet I do" (135).

More's passivity reminds the reader of Binx Bolling, another searcher who has difficulty making decisions and who seems dislocated from his family and his life.

We can see More's ontological standing most clearly in this scene at Pantherburn. After dinner Tom drinks in the dim dining room, trying to find relief from the existential burden of constant choice. He feels comfortable "drinking in the dark," mildly dissociated from his body and from the news Lucy has given him that his wife Ellen has tested positive for Herpes IV. Since he was at Fort Pelham when Ellen had the test, he knows that he is not the origin. More perfectly names his ontological position: "I stand in the dark. . . . It is not bad standing in the dark drinking" (159). Until Lucy enters the room, Tom does not even know whether he is sitting or standing. "There is this to be said for drinking," he muses, "It frees one from the necessities of time, like: now it is time to sit down, stand up. One would as soon do one thing as another" (159).

In this dissociated state, Tom eventually makes love to Lucy after she fetches him from the parlor, leads him up the stairs, and climbs into bed with him. Percy does not introduce intersubjectivity into this lovemaking scene. Tom sees Lucy not as an individual but as a composite woman: "She, Alabama-German-Lucy-Alice, is under the comforter and I under her, she a sweet heavy incubus but not quite centered" (163). Tom spends what he called in *Love in the Ruins* "a regular Walpurgis night" (*LR* 109), inhabited not by "witches, devils and pitchforks" but by the strangest combination of scenes from the past of Pantherburn and scenes set in Germany. The lovemaking is interspersed with dream–like fragments, which appear at first to be memories. He "remembers" the feather beds in Freiburg and waking "early in the morning to the sound of church bells" (162) and hiding in the woods with an old girlfriend, Alice Pratt, as a panzer division passed by on the road. There is an inescapable immediacy to these short scenes, and so the reader is as surprised as Tom himself appears to be when he tells Lucy the following morning, "I have never been to Germany" (166).

Tom's dreams bind him more tightly to Father Smith; the next day, Tom learns that Father Smith has had an hallucination the same night. When More receives word that Father Smith has suffered a "spell," he returns to the fire tower. Father Smith explains that something happened to him just after More left the day before and asks, "Is there something which is not a dream or even a daydream but the memory of an experience which is a thousand times more vivid than a dream but which happens in broad daylight when you are wide awake?" (235). The "hallucination" Father Smith recounts was of being back in Tübingen, where he lay in a feather bed and listened to church bells which "had a special quality, completely different from our church bells, a high-pitched, silvery sound, almost like crystal struck against crystal" (236). The details the priest remembers are very like those experienced by Tom More. Their dreams and lives are intermeshed, fused in such a way that Tom, who has few memories of his own, takes on some of Father Smith's.

The forces of death in *The Thanatos Syndrome* are led by Dr. Bob Comeaux, who is marked by his total devotion to a dangerous abstraction—the "quality of life." Percy's continuing interest in language both as it establishes an intersubjective world and as it can be used to distance and displace meaning, especially when abstractions hold sway, is apparent throughout the novel, most notably in his treatment of Bob Comeaux. Throughout his arguments with More, we see Comeaux equivocate, supply high-flown words for simpler, more descriptive ones, and generally prove to be a master of argumentation. From our first encounter with Bob, in his penthouse office in the Fedville complex, we see him as the consummate manager, a man "at the top now, director of something or other—Quality of Life Division, or something like" (23).

Percy perfectly captures the self-assured director whose speech falls into predictable patterns. Bob is comfortable with the standardized glib phrases of management, with the task-oriented jargon of a man who is "results-oriented" and above all pragmatic. He reveals himself in his language: "we're talking controlled substances," "we're talking a felony count" (27), "let's just put this business on hold" (28), "I'll get back to you" (28). He hurries his meeting with Tom and Max Gottlieb to its conclusion: "I'll give you a buzz. Any further questions? Max? Tom?" (29). Comeaux's studied way with his body reminds us of the gestural perfection that Binx Bolling so much admired in Hollywood actors, as Bob sits on his desk "swinging one leg and leaning over, hands in pockets"

(23–24). To reinforce his points and to establish contact, Bob lays his hand on Tom's shoulder (28), a gesture he repeats later at the awards banquet. More observes that Bob possesses "a new assurance" and he notices, more ominously, that Bob suffers the fate of Marcel's *poseur*, a self successfully posing as an invented self. More watches Bob and concludes that there is "a space between what he is and what he is doing. He is graceful and conscious of his gracefulness, like an actor" (26). Bob's wife Sheri remarks to Tom that she has always thought of him as the best doctor around, even better than her husband, "Dr. Perfect" (50), as she sarcastically refers to Bob in his hearing.

Clearly Bob Comeaux inhabits Marcel's realm of Having, where people are approached as problems to be solved rather than presences to be encountered. He loves to argue, to present points supporting euthanasia, trying to convince Tom that he is right. Noting Bob's penchant for argument, Tom muses: "Is he afraid that if one does not argue there is nothing left? An abyss opens. Is it not the case that something is better than nothing, arguing, violent disagreement, even war?" (35). Bob's need to justify his euthanasia program becomes even more apparent when Tom fails to answer him and Bob himself supplies the word that "pedeuthanasia" has been coined to replace:

> "In using the word *infanticide*, you see, you are dealing not with the issue but in semantics, a loaded semantics at that."
> "I didn't use the word" (36).

We sense Bob's uneasiness with his position, noticing how important it is to him to prove that he is doing the right thing. Bob encourages More to join his team: "Then be the devil's advocate. Attack us from your own expertise. Name one thing wrong we're doing" (193).

Even Bob Comeaux senses his need for the other, although he makes intersubjectivity impossible by refusing to *listen*. Comeaux reminds More of his fellow inmates at Fort Pelham: "After two years no one had convinced anyone else. Each side made the same points, the same rebuttals. Neither party listened to the other. They would come close as lovers, eyes glistening, shake fingers at each other, actually take hold of the other's clothes" (34). Even after

More has exposed the Blue Boy project and has convinced Comeaux to shut down the project and redirect the funds to Father Smith's hospice, Bob wants to defend what he has done. Again he challenges More: "Argue with the proposition that in the end there is no reason to allow a single child to suffer needlessly, a single old person to linger in pain, a single retard to soil himself for fifty years, suffer humiliation, and wreck his family," and he leaves Tom with a parting sally: "You can't give me one good reason why what I am doing is wrong" (346, 347). Before More has a chance to answer, Bob escapes. Even though he has temporarily defeated Bob, Tom still can't summon a refutation, and if Feliciana parish seems safe enough from the likes of Comeaux and Van Dorn, there are plenty of other places for them to set up operations. *Doe v. Dade*, the landmark Supreme Court decision which allows "gereuthanasia of the old or pedeuthanasia of pre-personhood infants," is still the law of the land (334).[8] When More fails to tell Comeaux that what he is doing is wrong, the reader feels compelled to jump into the void left by Tom and confront Bob's ideas directly.

As Aunt Emily assumed that Binx lived by the same values she held dear, so Bob Comeaux tells More that they "live by the same lights, share certain basic assumptions and goals" (190). He defines these goals for More in a sentence that rings with generalizations: "Healing the sick, ministering to the suffering, improving the quality of life for the individual regardless of race, creed, or national origin" (190). If we agree that language determines perception, which in turn is the basis of our beliefs and policies, then what Bob Comeaux is doing to language is dangerous indeed. Comeaux's talk is full of words like *neonate*, already in the dictionary, and *euthanate*, not yet a part of the language, but if euthanasia is ever widely accepted, we will need a noun for the euthanasia candidate. Back-formed from *euthanasia*, *euthanate* is a likely neologism. It is worth noting that the pattern is already there in medical language. In *The Mind*, Richard Restak writes that a person who develops the fatal disease kuru, found in New Guinea, is reduced in the final stages of the disease to a "helpless *dement*".[9] What happens when language makes room for such terms as "dement?" Is it still possible to see the demented individual, or has the person disappeared, subsumed, as Father Smith would say, under the label? Once *neonate* gains general acceptance, it successfully distances us from the individual infant, and once distanced, the "neonate" can be more easily disposed of. When this occurs, we cannot be far from accepting *pedeuthanasia* to name *infanticide*. The action becomes speakable. Percy understands that in addition to mirroring reality, language shapes new realities.

With the example of Bob Comeaux before us, we recall Percy's and Marcel's warnings about language, how easily words can lose contact with what they name. Thus the sparrow is deprived of being as soon as we utter the phrase "just a sparrow." Words wear out, and new words must be coined, and Percy is always aware that new words may be dangerous. Even "intersubjectivity," which names the primal relationship between an "I" and a "thou," can easily become devalued under certain circumstances. For example, Dr. More recoils when one of his patients, Debbie Boudreaux, a former Maryknoll nun now married to ex-priest Kev Kevin, utters the word. As used by Debbie, *intersubjectivity* is part and parcel of "her everlasting talk about dialoguing, creativity, community, intersubjectivity, centeredness (her favorite word, *centeredness*). And her new word, *empowerment*" (81). With bedfellows like these, *intersubjectivity* loses all connection to the I/thou relationship it names, becoming an abstraction like the others, a trendy word bandied about by ineffective therapists.

Language can be humankind's salvation when it is used to name a world with the other, but it may also be its doom. Bob Comeaux's conversation provides further evidence to support Percy's contention that science has everything to say about specimens insofar as they are representatives of classes of things, and nothing whatsoever to say about *individuals* insofar as it is their particular lives which are in question. Marcel points out that when experts talk of "life," they tend to forget their own involvement:

> I could express more exactly what I mean by saying that the experience of *my life*, which is so difficult to think precisely, in some way secretly irrigates, as it were, the confused notion I tend to form of life independently of any knowledge of biology. Moreover, the biologist seems to think he need not take any account at all of this communication or of this articulation. And to the degree that he is impressed by this attitude of the scientist, the man in the street comes

to block the communication in question. When speaking of life, he forgets his condition as a living being.[10]

Marcel argues that it is absurd to discuss life in general, that to do so assures that life will lose its sacred nature. His worst forebodings seem to have come to pass among Bob Comeaux and company. Father Smith sums up the danger for More: "If you put the two together, a lover of Mankind and a theorist of Mankind, what you've got now is Robespierre or Stalin or Hitler and the Terror, and millions dead for the good of Mankind" (129).

Comeaux, however, describes himself as "just a guy out to improve a little bit the quality of life for all Americans" (200). He believes that "pedeuthanasia" and gereuthanasia" are necessary to achieve the greatest good for the greatest number. Once again, Percy shows abstraction triumphant; in Bob Comeaux's scheme, subjectivity is suspect, as is any sense of the self of a person. When More suggests to Comeaux that Mickey LaFaye's strange behavior may be the result of a "cortical deficit, probably prefrontal," Bob Comeaux immediately backs off: "Very interesting. Okay, okay. Let's skip the metaphysics. You get into the prefrontal, you get into metaphysics" (97). Bob wants to stick with what can be touched and probed, with problems that he believes can be "treated" with chemicals. He shies away from what interests Tom More most, the human psyche that "is born to trouble as the sparks fly up" (13). Even More realizes the tenuous ground he is trying to hold: "If one can prescribe a chemical and overnight turn a haunted soul into a bustling little body, why take on such a quixotic quest as pursuing the secret of one's very self?" (13).

Bob Comeaux reduces individuals to the ontological status of specimens; they are seen as members of various *classes* but not *as individuals*. Ironically, even in Bob Comeaux's new Eden, where "quality of life" has become the first principle, individuals continue to have anxieties and commit crimes. Therefore, those healthy enough to be allowed to live must again be treated—and so Bob has spearheaded the Blue Boy project to add heavy sodium to the water supply. This is Bob's answer to crime, teenage pregnancies, drug addiction and child abuse. Bob can show with statistics the success of the Blue Boy project: admissions for violent crime to Angola, the State Prison Farm, have decreased 72 percent and the incidence in the prison population of "murder, knifings, and homosexual rape" has declined to zero (194).

And what of the "flatness of affect" that More has observed in his patients, what of their tendency to speak in telegraphic sentences like chimpanzees who have been taught to sign and who use words like counters?[11] The one negative result of the project, as Comeaux himself admits, is the diminishment in language, that intersubjective behavior which sets human beings apart from all other animals and which depends on context for true communication. More has noticed that his patients willingly answer questions, no matter how poorly the question fits the context of the conversation. He finds his patients "diminished" and notices especially what appears to be the loss of a sense of *self*. But Bob explains away More's objections by arguing that the new language best expresses the patients' nearly total recall of facts: "They're into graphic and binary communication—which after all is a lot more accurate than once upon a time there lived a wicked queen" (197). When More counters, "You mean they use two-word sentences," Bob explains that this is all that's necessary for them to produce the facts: "They can rattle off the total exports and imports of the port of Baton Rouge" (197). Tom's wife Ellen, for example, can figure out the exact probability of distribution after the first three tricks in a bridge game, but she has lost the ability to speak in complete sentences.

This reduction of the creature Percy has called *homo loquens* is especially horrifying. With language diminished, the human being is diminished, no longer able to reach out to others. With despair and anxiety removed by doses of heavy sodium, all uneasiness removed, the person's fundamental nature has been altered. In fact, this alteration has been a part of Bob Comeaux's conscious plan. We human beings have not been very well designed, Bob explains to More: "at least a segment of the human neocortex and of consciousness itself is not only an aberration of evolution but is also the scourge and curse of life on this earth, the source of wars, insanities, perversions—in short, those very pathologies which are peculiar to *Homo sapiens*" (195).

Thus, Comeaux replaces the Christian doctrine of original sin with a neurological explanation for the human propensity to err.

Once people have been given their daily sodium doses, they are relieved of all these difficulties. At home and adjusted to the environment like proper organisms, individuals cannot be wayfarers who understand their lives as a journey and who know that this earth is not their ultimate home. One of Percy's most deeply held beliefs is the importance of "being on the way," even if all that is possible is old-fashioned muddling through. He emphasizes the extraordinary staying power *homo viator* must demonstrate in the midst of a life that always comes without clear-cut directions. Percy's wayfarers are forever coming to themselves in a dark wood, as Dante would have it, occupying the human position T.S. Eliot describes: "In the middle, not only in the middle of the way/ But all the way, in a dark wood, in a bramble."[12] Tom More knows that life is mysterious; it does not move forward in an orderly manner but rather by "fits and starts, mostly fits" (75). Therefore Tom is concerned that—far from being wayfarers—the citizens of Feliciana are not clearly distinguishable from androids: the Stepford wives and husbands of late 20th century Louisiana.

Even John Van Dorn, who has hopes of accomplishing "the sexual liberation of civilization," thinks that Bob Comeaux and his colleagues are "cowboys" who lack ultimate goals. "You don't treat human ills by creaming the human cortex," Van Dorn explains to More, "That's a technologist for you. Give a technologist a new technique and he'll run with it like a special-team scatback" (217). Van Dorn, however, is even more villainous than Comeaux. He advocates sexual liberation primarily to indulge his own pedophilic tendencies, while claiming to have gotten to the origins of love and affection by initiating young children into sex. And despite his objections to Blue Boy, Van Dorn has participated in the project because "every society has the right to protect itself—even if it means temporary loss of civil liberties" (218–19). After a while spent listening to the likes of Comeaux and Van Dorn, inundated with the abuse of language, the reader is profoundly relieved when Sheriff Vernon "Cooter" Sharp speaks out loud and clear, pronouncing the final judgment on Van Dorn, the Brunettes, the Coach and Mrs. Chaney: "I mean, we got us some sick folks here" (322). How sane and exact his language is.

Temporarily taken with Comeaux's argument, More tells Father

Smith that "a society like an organism has a right to survive" (234). Father Smith latches on to the word *society* and mumbles something More cannot quite make out about *Volk*. In fact, it seems obvious that Father Smith tells More his story—included in the novel as a special section entitled "Father Smith's Confession"—of the Weimar doctors he encountered while visiting cousins in Germany in the thirties because he considers the information vitally important to his friend.

In order that Tom might see the threat that Bob Comeaux and his Fedville physicians present, Father Smith tells More that he was so attracted to the SS that if he had been German, he would have joined them. Bob Comeaux's argument that society is best served when "quality of life" becomes the prime directive reminds Father Smith of Dr. Brandt, one of the Weimar doctors who "maintained that 'reverence for nation' preceded 'reverence for life'" (246). Father Smith warns More that "Tenderness is the first disguise of the murderer" (128) and that it leads inevitably to the gas chamber. His statement has its roots in one of Flannery O'Connor's essays in *Mystery and Manners*. O'Connor clarifies the connection that Father Smith makes between tenderness and the gas chamber:

> If other ages felt less, they saw more, even though they saw with the blind, prophetical, unsentimental eye of acceptance, which is to say, of faith. In the absence of this faith now, we govern by tenderness. It is a tenderness which, long since cut off from the person of Christ, is wrapped in theory. When tenderness is detached from the source of tenderness, its logical outcome is terror. It ends in forced-labor camps and in the fumes of the gas chamber.[13]

The process bears examination. As it is specifically worked out in Father Smith's thinking, the inevitable chain of events begins with an individual, both lover and theorist of humankind, who finds a way to relieve the suffering of another person. Then, seeing the effect of this mercy, the individual feels pride in the results which have been achieved. Eventually the individual decides to define "quality of life," to determine whether another person, perhaps one afflicted with multiple birth defects, would not be better off dead than living so limited a life. The family of this individual, as Bob Comeaux would argue, will certainly be better off. The first to go are those with insuperable physical and mental problems. Eventually, full of hubris, and feeling like God's accomplice, the social engineer sees others who are in need of the ultimate solution to the miseries of their lives.[14]

Once the killing has begun, according to O'Connor and Percy, we have taken the first step down a slippery slope. The inevitable end is mass extermination. Father Smith reminds More that Hitler held the abstraction *Das Volk* above any consideration for individuals, thinking of the German people as an organism, one that was threatened by "impurities" such as those Slavs and Jews might introduce. According to Hitler's vision, the pure organism of *Das Volk* was best served if these "lesser" racial groups were eliminated. Father Smith tells More that even as a teenager he could follow Hitler's speeches well enough to get the drift: "I understood enough German to understand such words as *alien, decadent, foreign body* in the pure organism of the *Volk* (249).[15] What began as a program to assure the well-being of the German people soon led to the demand for a final solution to the Jewish problem.

Father Smith's comments echo a prominent Marcellian theme to which Percy returns time and again—the assertion that abstractions kill, that only the concrete saves. From his earliest grapplings with idealist philosophy, Marcel saw that the "life" which was under philosophical consideration was an abstraction which failed to include the individual's life, just as biologists talking of life never seemed to include themselves within the abstraction they undertook to explain. Thus a gulf opens between the concept and the individual, and *homo viator*'s being is in danger of being lost. Marcel writes:

> On many occasions I have denounced the fatal consequences of the spirit of abstraction . . . and have tried to show that that spirit leads to fanaticism, in other words, to idolatry, and that such idolatry is invariably accompanied by a paroxysm of objectivisation (this applies equally to Marxist materialism and Nazi racism) [*MJ* ix].

Marcel further warns that death simply becomes "objectively and functionally, the scrapping of what has ceased to be of use and must be written off as total loss" (*PE* 11–12). The modern world has, according to Marcel, all too willingly believed that technology has penetrated to the very secret of life, and the result has been a life that has "undergone a kind of general devaluation" (*TW* 107). Once a man like Bob Comeaux decides to engineer the lives of others, all life everywhere is in danger of breaking loose from its ontological moorings. Reduced from subject to object, the individual being in the world becomes an organism in an environment, to use one of Percy's recurring phrases. Individuals are reduced to the third person, for whom Bob Comeaux and the "Louisiana Weimar physicians" are more than willing to make plans.

Readers familiar with Percy's concerns with language will remember his particular interest in words as they mean and as they occasionally fail to mean, for language is tricky and it seems that just as we have got a thing or a concept named, it disappears behind its name, becoming a simulacrum of itself. When we see Father Smith in the fire tower, he can no longer preach because the words don't signify. However, as he explains to More, the action of the mass continues to signify (117). For him, the old words of grace have failed, but re-enacting the sacrifice of the incarnate Word continues to hold out hope for the participants. Driven to the point where the language of religion fails, and unable to provide new words, Father Smith elects to remain in the fire tower.

Although actions can speak more clearly than words, Percy stresses the difficulty of interpreting Father Smith's withdrawal from the world. For if words are slippery, actions can be just as difficult to read. Dr. More thinks that Father Smith may be protesting the closing of St. Margaret's hospice, due to the withdrawal of government funding. Young Father Placide comments: "I don't know whether Father Smith is a nut or a genius, or whether he has some special religious calling" (110). One of the church ladies, Jan Greene, suggests that Father Smith could be performing "vicarious penance for the awful state of the world" (113), and Ernestine Kelly suggests that Father Smith may be a saint, noting that two people have experienced miracles—a tumor healed, a lost son recovered—after they wrote their intentions and "pinned the notes to the steps of the tower" (112). Dan, a laconic deacon, suggests the most matter-of-fact conclusion of all: "Why make it complicated. . . . It's just a cop-out. There is such a thing. He quit, period. Who wouldn't like to quit and take to the woods?" (113–14). The final answer, insofar as one exists, seems to be that all these explanations may contain parts of the truth. In ascending out of the temporal world, Father Smith resembles his patron saint, Simeon the Stylite. Saint, alcoholic, madman, or perhaps just an elderly man suffering from temporal-brain epilepsy, Father Smith is caught up in a mystery in which Tom More finds himself increasingly involved.

Near the end of the novel, however, Percy allows Father Smith to preach a "sermon" to issue a warning. Although Percy believes that the main business of the novelist is to tell a story, "even a novelist has a right to issue a warning."[16] To avoid didacticism, Percy resorts to a most interesting indirect approach. On the occasion of the reopening of St. Margaret's Hospice, an event that marks the temporary defeat of the powers of darkness in Feliciana parish, Father Smith conducts a service on January 5, the feast day of his patron saint. As we have seen, Percy's novels frequently feature a priest at the end: Father Boomer in *The Last Gentleman*, Father Smith in *Love in the Ruins*, Father Weatherbee (interestingly the only non-Catholic cleric) in *The Second Coming*, and Father John, who listens silently until the final pages of *Lancelot*. But *The Thanatos Syndrome* is unique because, for the first time, Percy's priest is allowed to speak out clearly and passionately, judging his congregation and the larger community. Furthermore, the scene receives special emphasis because it provides the only opportunity to hear Father Smith speak outside his fire tower.

John Edward Hardy argues that Father Smith's sermon smacks strongly of "authorial *intrusion*," but he notes that upon second reading the "novelistic situation here looks a good deal more interestingly complicated."[17] The scene *is* deliberately complicated in its telling, and Percy's narrative method makes all the difference in reader reaction to Father Smith's remarks. Before presenting the sermon, Percy deliberately undermines the account; More comments that Father Smith "behaved so strangely that even I, who knew him best, could not make head or tail of what he was saying. . . . To make matters worse, he also managed to offend everyone, even those most disposed to help him and the hospice" (357).

Percy intricately complicates Father Smith's message by mediating it through More, the first person narrator. By providing Tom

More's running commentary on Father Smith's words and actions, Percy sets the reader at several removes from the priest's vehement outbursts. The reader is free to assume that the priest's words need not be taken seriously. It is important to notice that More's discomfort is magnified by the presence of a large audience composed of "local notables . . . priests, ministers, and a rabbi . . . [and] many of my fellow physicians both federal and local" (357). To make matters worse, the "News Team-7" remote unit is set up to tape the proceedings for the evening news. Father Smith looks strange: he has forgotten his vestments and wears "the rumpled chinos and sneakers he wore in the fire tower" (358); more ominously, More notices "a certain gleam in his eye, both knowing and rapt which I've seen before, in him and on closed wards" (358). More is embarrassed for the priest, partially because he has developed an intersubjective relationship with him. Just when it seems that Father Smith is about to say Mass, he turns and speaks:

> [I]nstead of mounting the single step to the platform of the altar, he turns around in the aisle, not two feet from me, exactly between me and Max, and faces the little crowd, which is still well disposed if somewhat puzzled.
>
> "Jesus Christ is Lord!" he says in a new, knowledgeable, even chipper voice. Then: "Praise be to God! Blessed be his Holy Name!" A pause and then, as he looks down at the upturned faces: "I wonder if you know what you are doing here!" (358).

We remember that Father Smith's retreat to the fire tower was occasioned by his belief that words no longer signify, that only the Mass continued to signify. On his saint's day, the priest tries once again to employ language to tell his audience—especially More (notice that he stands "not two feet" from Tom)—what they most need to hear. Percy constructs the scene so that Father Smith's intersubjective naming act combines with More's self-conscious narration of the priest's "ejaculations" to create for the readers a space where the old words may be heard anew, not in spite of but *because of* the ironic context. Attentive readers will notice that they stand indicted along with the congregation. The telling of the tale undermines it; we neglect to put up defenses, and Father Smith's words have a chance to reach us. His outbursts—"I don't see any sinners here," "Look at you. Not a sinner in sight," "What a generation! Believing thieves and decent unbelievers," "But beware, tender hearts!" (360–61)—reach the reader as disconnected fragments. What we have finally, then, is not a sermon but a gestalt of Father Smith's most deeply felt observations on human behavior.

Percy's indirect presentation of Father Smith's "sermon" is diametrically opposed to Bob Comeaux's direct argumentative method. Bob uses facts and figures to support his positions, whereas Father Smith delivers disconnected judgments which demand that readers take on the responsibility for examining the accusations. The scene is contrived to provide every opportunity for the reader to listen to both More *and* the priest, to become a member of Father Smith's congregation and to respond as a "thou." Percy successfully broadens the intersubjective nexus in this scene at St. Margaret's.

Set exactly one year after Father Smith's sermon, Section 14 contains the final two scenes of the novel: Father Smith's call to Tom to assist at Mass and Tom's session with Mickey LaFaye, who is now free of heavy sodium and once again full of anxiety and eager to talk.[18] In these two scenes, two hopes are extended to Tom More: the possibility of spiritual intersubjectivity, an I/Thou relationship with God, which Father Smith pursues; and the possibility that by talking and especially listening, Dr. More will be able to help his patients. In the first of the two scenes, Ellen relays Father Smith's telephone call, telling Tom that the priest mentioned "Royalty, a visit, gifts and—a Jewish connection" (369). Ellen supplies her own context for Father Smith's message (at least she is sufficiently recovered from the effects of heavy sodium to *have* a context), guessing that Father Smith's "important referral" might be Queen Margarita of Spain. Then Ellen comments, in words that are certainly double: "I think it's a valuable connection for you" (370). So long as More continues his relationship with Father Smith, there is hope that the essential nature of Christ as Incarnate Word will be made manifest to him, and that he will see that the intersubjective therapy he provides for his patients is an earthly model of the relationship with God which Father Smith embodies.

One critic observes that Percy has ended all his novels "unexpectedly with a miracle of sorts, actually with an epiphany—God appears."[19] *The Thanatos Syndrome* ends with the approach of the actual Epiphany. Ellen is wrong about the priest's message; his references to "Royalty . . . and a Jewish connection" are his code for the coming Feast of the Epiphany. It is especially significant that More agrees to assist Father Smith in this celebration. One of the oldest of Christian festivals, Epiphany commemorates the manifestation of Christ to the nations. Until the arrival of the magi, the birth of Jesus was a decidedly provincial matter, with implications perhaps for the Jewish community but with no adumbrations in the larger world. When the foreign kings arrived in Bethlehem and offered gifts to the baby, representatives of the Gentile world acknowledged Christ's essential nature. Tom's willingness to aid Father Smith in this particular mass indicates that grace may yet lead him to his own epiphany.

The last scene of the novel, More's session with his old patient, Mickey LaFaye, demonstrates the importance of talking and listening and emphasizes a way to live in the natural, temporal world. More continues to practice psychiatry with Father Smith's approval: "Do what you are doing. You are on the right track. Continue with the analysis and treatment of your patients. . . . I have watched you. Carry on. Keep a good heart" (366). Father Smith is affirming one of Percy's most deeply held convictions, that in the lower case I/thou relationship, specifically manifested in the act of naming which opens a shared consciousness of the world, God is present—as the absolute Thou whose creation is celebrated in the naming act and whose love is made manifest in the earthly subjects.

Tom More no longer looks for signs of the end in *The Thanatos Syndrome*.[20] In fact, More announces that he doesn't know what he believes. Millenarian thoughts are restricted to Father Smith, who lives in the fire tower, cut off physically but not spiritually from those below. Commenting on *Love in the Ruins*, Hardy discusses Father Smith's part-time job as firewatcher, noting that looking for signs of the end of the world is the priest's appropriate work and not Tom More's.[21] At the end of *Thanatos*, then, we have an appropriate division of labor: Father Smith will remain in his tower, looking for signs of earthly fires and of the fire foretold in

Revelation, and More will work with his patients, going about his ordinary duties, and like Binx Bolling, he will "listen to people, see how they stick themselves into the world, hand them along a ways in their dark journey and be handed along, and for good and selfish reasons" (*M* 233). Percy is thus redefining Binx Bolling's horizontal and vertical searches. Tom More pursues Binx's horizontal search as he listens to his patients, trying to get at "the root of trouble, the soul's own secret, by venturing into the heart of darkness . . . by talking and listening, mostly listening, to another troubled human being" (13). Father Smith pursues a vertical search—no longer one which is doomed to abstraction because it addresses the problems of the universe while failing to say anything about the individual—but newly defined as a transcendent movement toward God, who can only be thought of as an absolute Thou, and about whom, according to Marcel, we cannot think in the third person.[22]

Father Smith remains in his fire tower in order to be in a position to issue a warning if signs of the end do present themselves, his mission only slightly undercut by the fact that at times he appears slightly crazed. He is, after all, in a long tradition of men and women whose holiness seems madness to ordinary mortals. Of Father Smith's patron saint, St. Simeon Stylites, Percy remarks, "God does strange things. . . . he picked as one of his saints a fellow in northern Syria, a local nut, who stood on top of a pole for thirty-seven years."[23] The tasks of watching and waiting and of participating in the immanent world have been divided between Father Smith and Tom More, who have all along been a formidable twosome.

Perhaps most significantly, by the end of the novel language has been restored, even to Father Smith. As novelist, Percy must restore a belief in language. Percy has said that one of the novelist's responsibilities is to provide new language by which to name being. Percy has spoken of the novelist's responsibility to renew language many times, most recently in an interview: "Words are like the original sin, the fall of man. Father Smith says you can't use the words any more; the Great Depriver has deprived the words of meaning. But the novelist is a crafty and devious individual, so he has his own way of dealing with these things. One of his tasks is the renewal of words."[24] We see the rejuvenation of language in Father

Smith's resumption of language—at least to send messages to More when he needs his assistance—and in More's rededication to listening and to helping his patients speak the unspeakable so that they may come to know themselves.

We find Tom More in his office in the last scene, listening once more to Mickey LaFaye. As Mickey LaFaye begins to talk, Dr. More thinks to himself, "Well well well," the final words of the novel indicating that wellness may be brought about by the shared consciousness of More and his patient, the fissure between the "I" and the "thou" closed by the word.

Afterword

In May 1989, Walker Percy addressed a packed house in the Commerce Department Auditorium in Washington, D.C., as he delivered the eighteenth National Endowment for the Humanities Jefferson Lecture. During this lecture, "The Fateful Rift: The San Andreas Fault in the Modern Mind," Percy mentioned Heidegger and Sartre as philosophers whose ideas had particularly influenced his thinking, and several times he paid homage to Gabriel Marcel. Once again, Percy stressed Marcel's characterization of the human being as *homo viator* and suggested that we must look to philosophy and to language—that uniquely human phenomenon—to develop a new science of humankind to replace the "over 600 different schools of psychotheraphy" which now hold sway. To develop a coherent science of humankind, Percy said, we would be wise to consider the contributions of phenomenology—Marcel's assertion that the individual is "radically dependent upon others," for instance, is essential.

Clearly, Marcel's worldview, his phenomenological studies of such human conditions as fidelity, despair and hope, and his embodiment of philosophical concepts in the concrete situations of human life have been especially important to Percy. In Percy's novels, it is only when subjects encounter each other as "thous," presences who are open and available to each other, that any sort of meaningful life is possible. Love begins with the individual's ability to recognize the other as "I myself," with all the subjectivity that the individual knows the self to have. The bond that is created between the I and the thou is the requirement for any sort of ontological security in our fragmented and uncentered world.

From the beginning of his career as a novelist, Percy's focus has been on the problem of just *how* the individual learns about self and others. As we have seen, *The Moviegoer* presents all the basic elements of the intersubjective relationship: an openness and availability to the other, the sharing of language and the naming process, and a certain humbleness before Being. From *The Moviegoer*, in which Binx finally accepts responsibility for Kate, to *The Thanatos Syndrome*, in which Percy most clearly demonstrates the danger of abstractions which threaten the individual's constitution of self, Percy affirms the centrality of the I/thou communion. The pattern of the novels suggests a continual return to the mystery of self and other.

Read in the order of their publication, Percy's novels move from a rendering of the single alienated consciousness toward the full portrayal of both I and thou, which culminates in *The Second Coming*. While the earlier novels point toward a completely intersubjective relationship, this novel actually achieves it, presenting the relationship to us from both sides. The "other" as represented in Kate Cutrer, Sutter Vaught, Ellen Oglethorpe and Father John in the first four novels is manifested in Allie Huger. We are able to see the needs of both Will Barrett and Allie, able to understand the personal alienation of each, and thus realize the power of their developing intersubjective communion. Then, in *The Thanatos Syndrome*, Percy again presents both I and thou in Tom More and Father Smith. In two sections where Father Smith becomes the first person narrator—"Father Smith's Confession" and "Father Smith's Footnote"—More's narration is displaced, and Percy calls attention to the spiritual plane where the decisions being made in Fedville do not make sense. In essence, the silent priest of *Lancelot* comes forward to speak for himself in *The Thanatos Syndrome*, which has been called Percy's most Catholic novel.

It is here, in *The Thanatos Syndrome*, that Percy most clearly involves the *readers* in an intersubjective relationship. As we have seen, he offers multiple explanations for Father Smith's towersitting, allowing readers to draw their own conclusions about the priest. Father Smith is ironically undermined throughout the novel. Is he, after all, simply a confused old man whose action (ascending into the fire tower) and words (his "sermon") simply do not signify anything beyond his own condition? Percy leaves the matter open, trusting that some of his readers will become the others to whom he wants to speak. These particular readers, like Tom More, will have to decipher Father Smith's message and reconsider their own positions in the modern world. They may, as Percy would say, by the grace of God, hear and decipher the message in the bottle.

For all the novels are vessels—bottles—containing ironically encoded messages, news which Percy believes modern individuals need to hear. The reader is affirmed as a presence, as a potential "thou" whose participation in the novel is essential to giving the text meaning. The author and reader must come to agree on the system of naming which has been developed. These novels operate through a call, a vocation of self that Percy strives to elicit from his readers. Not only is intersubjectivity one of Percy's primary themes—*it is also the very mode of being which his novels demand.* The relationship between the text and the reader of that text is intersubjective. Percy's call to the self of the other seeks to break down our defenses, undermine all our stratagems and impersonations, and make it possible for the word to penetrate.

Percy has long argued that art, like science, is cognitive. The serious novelist is committed to telling the truth of being. When the truth we seek has to do with what it is like to live in the twentieth century, the novelist can tell us what the scientist cannot. Science can provide only general truths, whereas the artist reveals "the human being . . . [who] is stuck with the consciousness of himself as a self, as a unique individual, or at least with the possibility of becoming such a self."[1] The individual, accepting personal sovereignty, asks questions about what it means to live a life. According to Percy, the novelist provides tentative anwers:

> It is the artist who at his best reverses the alienating process by the very act of seeing it clearly for what it is and naming it, and who in this same act establishes a kind of community. It is a paradoxical community whose members are both alone yet not alone, who strive to become themselves and discover that there are others who, however tentatively, have undertaken the same quest.[2]

Thus Percy imagines an intersubjective relationship developing between the novel and its readers, individuals involved in this sort of "quest," people who are seeking others who are similarly engaged. The writer, the giver of names, assists in this quest:

If he [the writer] is a good poet and names something which we secretly and privately know but have not named, we rejoice at the naming and say, Yes! I know what you mean! Once again we are co-celebrants of being. This joy is as cognitive and as ontological as the joy of a hypothesis. It is a perversion of art to look upon science as the true naming and knowing and upon art as a traffic in emotions. Both science and art discover being, and neither may patronize the other.[3]

The relationship between author, text and reader is complicated and deeply intersubjective in nature, involving as it does the author's naming act, the named things (the text) and the reader's response to what has been named. One can reject or accept, open up to what the text contains, or close down, unwilling to encounter or accept such threatening or self-revealing ideas. We do not always want to have our unnameable selves named for us by another. Percy's novels are imaginative constructs of life and not life itself, certainly; yet the lives of Binx, Will, Tom and even Lancelot *could* be real, and it is possible to see ourselves in them. If we choose to accept this, the six novels provide a ground on which we can encounter our own metaphysical uneasiness. They may make our own subjectivity available to us.

Works Cited

BY GABRIEL MARCEL

Metaphysical Journal   (*MJ*)
    Trans. Bernard Wall. Chicago: Regnery, Gateway
    ed., 1952.

Being and Having: An Existentialist Diary   (*BH*)
    Trans. Katherine Farrer. New York: Harper, 1965.

Homo Viator: Introduction to a Metaphysic of Hope   (*HV*)
    Trans. Emma Craufurd, New York: Harper,
    1962.

The Philosophy of Existentialism   (*PE*)
    Trans. Manya Harari. New York: Citadel, 1956.

The Mystery of Being, 2 vols.
vol. 1: *Reflection and Mystery*   (*MB* 1)
    Trans. G.S. Fraser. Chicago: Regnery, Gateway
    ed., 1960.
vol. 2: *Faith and Reality*   (*MB* 2)
    Trans. Rene Hague, Chicago: Regnery, Gateway
    ed., 1960.

Creative Fidelity   (*CF*)
    Trans. Robert Rosthal. New York: Farrar, 1964.

Tragic Wisdom and Beyond   (*TW*)
    Trans. Stephen Jolin and Peter McCormick.
    Evanston: Northwestern University Press, 1973.

The Existential Background of Human Dignity.   (*EBHD*)
   Cambridge: Harvard University Press, 1963.

BY WALKER PERCY

Novels

   The Moviegoer   (*M*)
     New York: Farrar, Noonday, 1967.

   The Last Gentleman   (*LG*)
     New York: Farrar, Noonday, 1966.

   Love in the Ruins   (*LR*)
     New York: Farrar, Noonday, 1971.

   Lancelot   (*L*)
     New York: Farrar, 1977.

   The Second Coming   (*SC*)
     New York: Farrar, 1980.

   The Thanatos Syndrome   (*TS*)
     New York: Farrar, 1987.

Books of Essays

   *The Message in the Bottle: How Queer Man is, How
   Queer Language Is, and What One Has to Do with the
   Other*   (*Message*)
     New York: Farrar, Noonday, 1977.

   Lost in the Cosmos: The Last Self-Help Book
     New York: Farrar, 1983.

Notes

Notes to Chapter One

1. Lewis A. Lawson and Victor A. Kramer, eds., *Conversations with Walker Percy* (Jackson: University Press of Mississippi, 1985) 263.

2. Lawson and Kramer, *Conversations* 263. Saranac Lake was the site of a number of changes in people's lives. William Howarth, in a review of Robert Taylor's *Saranac: America's Magic Mountain*, notes that many patients underwent "conversions" while staying at Saranac Lake: "Like the magic mountain in Thomas Mann's novel, Saranac transforms many of its pilgrims. They ascend, withdraw from normal routines, and often mark a turning point in life." [*The Washington Post Book World* 14 (Sunday, 6 April 1986) 7.]

3. John C. Carr, "An Interview with Walker Percy" (1971) in Lawson and Kramer, *Conversations* 59.

4. Linda Whitney Hobson, "The Study of Consciousness: An Interview with Walker Percy" in Lawson and Kramer, *Conversations* 223.

5. For Percy's use of Kierkegaardian themes, see Lewis A. Lawson, "Walker Percy's Indirect Communications," *Texas Studies in Language and Literature* 11 (1969): 867–900, which provides a close study of *The Moviegoer* and *The Last Gentleman*. Percy's indebtedness to Kierkegaard is also demonstrated in Robert Coles's *Walker Percy: An American Search* in his chapter on Percy's philosophical roots, 3–49. Although Coles argues that Kierkegaard is Percy's primary forebear, he provides thoughtful discussion of Marcel's importance to Percy. Martin Luschei investigates Percy's reading of the existentialists, especially Kierkegaard, Heidegger and Marcel in *The Sovereign Wayfarer: Walker Percy's Diagnosis of the Malaise* (Baton Rouge: Louisiana State University Press, 1972) 19–63. Luschei finds Percy closest to Marcel in his view of the human being (35). John F. Zeugner addresses Marcellian themes in *The Moviegoer* and *The Last Gentleman* in "Walker Percy and Gabriel Marcel: The Castaway and the Wayfarer," *Mississippi Quarterly* 28 (1974): 21–53. Zeugner's discussion is often confusing as, for example, when he states "the human entity deprived of intersubjectivity, would live as a wayfarer . . . or castaway in life." According to Marcel, the individual is both wayfarer *and* intersubjective presence in the world. Zeugner also intimates that "intersubjectivity" and "salvation" are different categories, whereas Marcel clearly shows that one's relationship with God is intersubjective, because God can only be thought of as the "absolute Thou."

6. Harriet Doar, "Walker Percy: He Likes to Put Protagonist in Situation" in Lawson and Kramer, *Conversations* 5.

7. Don L. Keith, "Walker Percy Talks of Many Things" in Lawson and Kramer, *Conversations* 9.

8. Carlton Cremeens, "Walker Percy, The Man and the Novelist" in Lawson and Kramer, *Conversations* 31. Percy is particularly taken with Marcel's designation of the individual as *homo viator*. Percy describes the human being as "a strange creature whom both Thomas Aquinas and Marcel called *homo viator*, man the wanderer" (John C. Carr, "An Interview with Walker Percy" in Lawson and Kramer, *Conversations* 64.) When Gilbert Schricke tells Percy that he is going to give a talk on Gabriel Marcel, Percy responds, "Apart from the Russians, three French writers had the greatest influence on me: Camus, Sartre and Gabriel Marcel. I studied them a lot" (Lawson and Kramer, *Conversations* 245–46). In an interview with Zoltan Abadi-Nagy, Percy says: "I identify philosophically with people like Gabriel Marcel. And if you want to call me a philosophical Catholic existentialist, I would not object, although the term existentialist is being so abused now that it means very little" (Lawson and Kramer, *Conversations* 73).

9. "Walker Percy Talks about Kierkegaard: An Annotated Interview" in Lawson and Kramer, *Conversations* 119.

10. Walker Percy, "Symbol as Need" in *The Message in the Bottle: How Queer Man Is, How Queer Language Is, and What One Has to Do with the Other* (New York: Farrar, Noonday, 1977) 295. Future references are to this edition, abbreviated as *Message*.

11. Gabriel Marcel, *The Mystery of Being, vol 2: Faith and Reality*, trans. Rene Hague (Chicago: Regnery, Gateway ed., 1960) 10. Future references to this edition abbreviated as *MB* 2, appear parenthetically in the text.

12. The phrase is Gilbert Ryle's description of the Cartesian *cogito*. See Lewis A. Lawson, "Tom More: Cartesian Physician," *Delta* 13 (Nov. 1981): 72. Walker Percy agrees with Marcel's anti-cartesian stance. In "Symbol as Hermeneutic in Existentialism," Percy announces his rejection of the *cogito* in a passage that shows his indebtedness to Marcel: "Both the empiricists and the existentialists (excepting Marcel) are wrong in positing an autonomous consciousness. . . . The decisive stroke against the myth of the autonomous Kantian subject is the intersubjective constitution of consciousness. There is a mutuality between the I and the Thou and the object which is in itself prime and irreducible. Once, in theorizing, this relation is ruptured, it cannot be recovered thereafter—witness the failure of both Sartre and the empiricists to give an account of intersubjectivity" (*Message* 282–83).

13. *Message* 115. In an interview with Marcus Smith, Percy mentions Marcel's assertion that language wears out: "There's nothing new about this, it's been noted before by people like Marcel—but language undergoes a period of degredation, words wear out" (Lawson and Kramer, *Conversations* 136).

14. Gabriel Marcel, *The Philosophy of Existentialism*, trans. Manya Harari (New York: Citadel, 1956) 121. Future references to this edition, abbreviated as *PE*, appear parenthetically in the text.

15. Gabriel Marcel, *The Existential Background of Human Dignity* (Cambridge: Harvard University Press, 1963) 36–37. Future references to this edition, abbreviated as *EBHD*, appear parenthetically in the text.

16. Early in *The Moviegoer*, Binx comments: "My wallet is full of identity cards, library cards, credit cards. Last year I purchased a flat olive-drab strongbox, very smooth and heavily built with double walls for fire protection, in which I

placed my birth certificate, college diploma, honorable discharge, G. I. insurance, a few stock certificates" (6–7).

17. *Walker Percy: A Southern Wayfarer* (Jackson: University Press of Mississippi, 1986) 25.

18. Gabriel Marcel, *Being and Having: An Existentialist Diary*, trans. Katherine Farrer (New York: Harper, 1965) 199. Future references to this edition, abbreviated as *BH*, appear parenthetically in the text.

19. See Herbert Spiegelberg's chapter on Marcel in *The Phenomenological Movement: A Historical Introduction*, 2 vols. (The Hague: Martinus Nijhoff, 1969), 421–44. Spiegelberg provides an excellent introduction to Marcel's thought. He points out Marcel's insistence that the reader participate in the philosophical search for meaning. Spiegelberg also takes note of the importance of Marcel's personality as a unifying factor in his philosophy.

20. Gabriel Marcel, *Metaphysical Journal*, trans. Bernard Wall (Chicago: Regnery, Gateway ed., 1952) 243. Future references to this edition, abbreviated as *MJ*, appear parenthetically in the text. Marcel discusses "my body" at length in *Metaphysical Journal* 242–280 and in *The Mystery of Being* 1: 113–135.

21. Walker Percy, *The Moviegoer* (New York: Farrar, Noonday, 1967) 11.

22. Walker Percy, *Love in the Ruins* (New York: Farrar, 1971) 97.

23. Walker Percy, *Lancelot* (New York: Farrar, 1977) 209.

24. Marcel originally published this essay as an appendix to his play, *Le Monde cassé*. It also appears in *The Philosophy of Existentialism* 9–46.

25. Marcel's entry of 22 October 1932 in *Being and Having* contains his first distinction between problem and mystery: "The phrase 'mystery of being, ontological mystery' as against the 'problem of being, ontological problem' has suddenly come to me in these last few days." A few days later, Marcel writes himself an instruction: "Distinguish between the Mysterious and the Problematic" (*BH* 100). A little later, in his entry for 7 November 1932, Marcel employs the term "metaproblematic" to describe the sphere where mystery operates. Up to this point, Marcel uses "problem" to refer to both problem and mystery. From this point on, he employs the term "mystery" whenever ontological questions are at issue.

26. *Disponibilité* is generally translated as "availability." Marcel comments on the term in *The Mystery of Being*: "The French terms I use are *disponibilité* and *indisponibilité*. Literally, in English, one would render these as *availability* and *unavailability*, but it might sound more natural if one spoke of handiness and unhandiness, the basic idea being that of having or not having, in a given contingency, one's resources to hand. The self-centered person, in this sense, is unhandy . . . he remains incapable of responding to calls made upon him by life. . . . He remains shut up in himself, in the petty circle of his private experience, which forms a kind of hard shell round him that he is incapable of breaking through" (*MB* 1: 201). Marcel's concept of *indisponibilité* figures prominently in Percy's novels. His main characters must struggle against their tendency to shut themselves off from the world of others.

27. *Lancelot* 100.

28. Walker Percy, *The Second Coming* (New York: Farrar, 1980) 233.

29. Gabriel Marcel, *The Mystery of Being, vol 1: Reflection and Mystery*, trans. G.S. Fraser (Chicago: Regnery, Gateway ed., 1960) 265. Future references to this

edition, abbreviated as *MB* 1, appear parenthetically in the text.

30. Gabriel Marcel, *Homo Viator: Introduction to a Metaphysic of Hope*, trans. Emma Craufurd (New York: Harper, 1962) 13. Future references to this edition, abbreviated as *HV*, appear parenthetically in the text.

31. "Symbol, Consciousness, and Intersubjectivity," in *Message* 275.

32. Like Marcel, Walker Percy is extremely interested in language and in naming as the prime intersubjective act. Often in Percy's novels when two individuals are not ontologically at ease with each other, their dis-ease is reflected in their inability to communicate with language, as is the case in *The Last Gentleman* when Will and Kitty attempt to make love in Central Park. The opposite situation, where intersubjectivity is fully operative, is embodied in Will and Allie's successful communications toward the end of *The Second Coming*.

33. Marcel notes the difference between *thou* and *Thou*: "While an empirical '*thou*' can be converted into a '*him*', God is the absolute '*thou*' who can never become a '*him*'" (*MJ* 137). God, then, is always a subject who can never be changed into an object. According to Marcel, God, who is pure Being, cannot be described as *having* attributes: "I feel that important metaphysical conclusions may be drawn from this, notably with regard to the impossibility of thinking of God according to the mode of Having, as *possessing*. In this sense any doctrine of the Attributes would tend inevitably to lead us astray. The *I am that I am* of Scripture would be truly the most adequate formula from an ontological point of view" (*BH* 147). Marcel says that God can only be approached as a Person, not as a prime mover or a transcendental cause. Because God is a living God, believers cannot "prove" His existence; believers can only testify to their faith in God.

34. In a letter to the author dated 25 August 1980, Percy says that most of his Marcel books were published in 1951 and that *Homo Viator* is "the most heavily marked-up and margin-noted of any." In the bibliography of *The Message in the Bottle*, Percy lists *Being and Having* and *The Mystery of Being*, both published in English in 1951. The English translation of *Metaphysical Journal* was also published in 1951. Since Percy shows a thorough grounding in Marcel's philosophy in his first published essay, "Symbol as Need" (1954), we can conclude that Percy first read Marcel between 1951 and 1953.

35. William Alexander Percy, *Lanterns on the Levee: Recollections of a Planter's Son* (Baton Rouge: Louisiana State University Press, 1973) x. Future references to this edition, abbreviated as *LL*, appear parenthetically in the text. Walker Percy wrote the introduction for this new edition. Not a full-scale autobiography, *Lanterns on the Levee* is a collection of elegiac reminiscences of the Mississippi delta, Will Percy's service in World War I, his father LeRoy's fight against Vardaman and the Ku Klux Klan. Anyone interested in the man who most deeply influenced Walker Percy will find many clues in this remarkable memoir, originally published in 1941 by Alfred A. Knopf.

36. The biographical details are taken from Lewis Baker, *The Percys of Mississippi: Politics and Literature in the New South* (Baton Rouge: Louisiana State University Press, 1983).

37. See *A Southern Renaissance: The Cultural Awakening of the American South, 1930–1955* (New York: Oxford University Press, 1980).

38. "The Delta Factor" in *Message* 4. Percy continues: "Why is it that the only time he was happy before was in the Argonne Forest in 1918 when he was shooting at Germans and stood a good chance of being shot by Germans? Why

was he sad from 1918 to 1941 even though he lived in as good an environment as man can devise, indeed had the best of all possible worlds in literature, music, and art?"

39. "Stoicism in the South," *Commonweal* 44 (1956): 344.

40. Walker Percy, *The Thanatos Syndrome* (New York: Farrar, 1987) 257.

41. "Notes for a Novel About the End of the World," in *Message* 112.

Notes to Chapter Two

1. Walker Percy, *The Moviegoer* (New York: Farrar, Noonday, 1967) 94. Future references to this edition appear parenthetically in the text.

2. So cut off from others is Binx that he cannot imagine a future that will differ from his present. Binx is in the situation of the person without hope that Marcel discusses in *Homo Viator*. According to Marcel, the individual who is spiritually unavailable to others lives "as though the future, drained of its substance and its mystery, were no longer to be anything but a place of pure repetition. . . . a future thus devitalized, no longer being a future for me or anybody else, would be rather a prospect of vacancy" (*HV* 60). Observing that three of his acquaintances have recently named their daughters Stephanie, Binx imagines a future just like the present. Only the name of his secretary will change: "Twenty years from now I shall perhaps have a rosy young Stephanie perched at my typewriter" (8).

3. Percy is commenting on Barbara King's assertion that Binx's life is one of "calculated despair" (Lawson and Kramer, *Conversations* 89).

4. Lewis Lawson concentrates on Percy's use of Kierkegaard in "Walker Percy's Indirect Communications," *Texas Studies in Literature and Language* 11 (Spring 1969): 867–900. The essay is reprinted in Lewis A. Lawson, *Following Percy: Essays on Walker Percy's Work* (Troy, NY: Whitston, 1988).

5. See William Rodney Allen, *Walker Percy: A Southern Wayfarer* (Jackson: University Press of Mississippi, 1986) 27–34, 40–41. Allen sheds light on the importance of Binx's search for his father. He contends that Binx's "double movement toward a closer relationship with Kate and the rediscovery of his feelings for his father" signals his progress toward a more authentic life (29).

6. See, for example, Percy's essays "Symbol as Need," 288–297 and "The Man on the Train," 83–100 in *The Message in the Bottle* and "Naming and Being" in *The Personalist* 41 (1960): 148–157.

7. Percy's close reading of Marcel is apparent in his echoing of *simulacrum*, one of Marcel's favorite words. In "Naming and Being," an essay published a year before *The Moviegoer*, Percy states, "Being is elusive; it tends to escape, leaving only a simulacrum of symbol" (*The Personalist* 41 (1960): 154). The word also appears in *The Moviegoer*. Describing his recurring dream of Korea, Binx says, "Again this morning the dream of war, not quite a dream but the simulacrum of a dream" (64). Binx's mother is also guilty of creating simulacra of people. Binx notes that when his mother discusses his father, she substitutes a simulacrum for the man: "My mother's recollection of my father is storied and of a piece. It is not him she remembers but an old emblem of him" (152).

8. The one exception to this rule is Lonnie Smith, Binx's half-brother, the one person Binx seems to love, but Lonnie is more a symbolic figure than a person. Lonnie can be seen as a forerunner to Allie Huger in *The Second Coming*, a person

who embodies grace. Binx finds communication with Lonnie possible because Lonnie speaks in a monotone and "his words are not worn out" (62). Binx is even able to tell Lonnie that he loves him because when Lonnie speaks: "It is like a code tapped through a wall. Sometimes he asks me straight out: do you love me? and it is possible to tap back: yes, I love you" (162). In the epilogue of *The Moviegoer*, Lonnie's death is made to carry great significance. Percy's development as a novelist can be seen by contrasting Lonnie Smith with Allie Huger; Lonnie lacks the life that Percy breathes into Allie.

9. See Lewis A. Lawson, "Walker Percy's Southern Stoic," *Southern Literary Journal* 3 (Fall 1970): 5–31; and "*The Moviegoer* and The Southern Heritage," in *The Stoic Strain in American Literature: Essays in Honour of Marston LaFrance*, ed. Duane J. MacMillan (Toronto: University of Toronto Press, 1979) 179–191. Both essays are reprinted in *Following Percy*.

10. The connection between romanticism and scientific objectivity, both systems that involve transcendence from the ordinary world where life is lived, is one that Percy explores in all his novels, most notably in the character of Sutter Vaught in *The Last Gentleman*. Sutter goes so far as to lay the decline of the West at the door of the Romantics. He tells Will Barrett: "It wasn't Marx or immorality or the Communists or the atheists or any of those fellows [who caused the decline of the western world]. It was Leigh Hunt" (*LG* 217).

11. Marcel understood the modern tendency to look at our own lives through the reigning model of scientific objectivity. For example, in *The Mystery of Being*, Marcel says: "It is of the very nature of our situation that it can be grasped only from within its own depths. But at the same time . . . in a world like our own, which is becoming more and more completely subjected to the dominion of objective knowledge and scientific technique, everything, by an almost fatal necessity, tends to fall out as if this observation of our situation from the outside were a real possibility" (*MB* 1: 250).

12. *Creative Fidelity*, trans. Robert Rosthal (New York: Farrar, 1964) 12. Future references to this edition, abbreviated as *CF*, appear parenthetically in the text.

13. In "The Man on the Train," Percy notes that "an intersubjective discovery of alienation is already its opposite" because anything that can be named and shared with another person is less fearsome than the original unnamed anxiety (*Message* 97).

14. See Percy's discussion of the radical loss of being which a specimen undergoes in "The Loss of the Creature" in *Message* 97.

15. "Symbol as Hermeneutic in Existentialism" in *Message* 285.

16. *Message* 285.

17. Throughout the novel, Binx frequents this parochial school playground near his house. It is significant that Binx waits for Kate in the playground because Marcel uses a playground metaphor to describe the spectator. Marcel argues that the spectator "makes as if to participate without really participating; he has emotions which are superficially similar to those of people who really are committed to some course of action or another, but he knows very well that in his case such emotions have no practical outcome. In other words he is the playground for a game of make-believe or let's pretend" (*MB* 1: 150–51).

18. Binx's audience here is very important. In Chicago Binx introduced Kate as his fiancé, but he was speaking to strangers. When he names Kate as his fiancé for the woman with whom he has just been flirting, he demonstrates Marcel's fidelity.

19. See, for example, Marcel's discussion in *The Mystery of Being*: "I concern

myself with being only insofar as I have a more or less distinct consciousness of the underlying unity which ties me to other beings of whose reality I already have a preliminary notion. . . . I should say of these beings that they are above all my fellow-travellers—my fellow-*creatures*" (*MB* 2: 19–20).

20. Aunt Emily's stoicism is particularly evident in her words to the eight-year-old Binx. In her system, death comes as the end to a long struggle; she cannot offer love or consolation to Binx, only advice on how to behave: "Scotty is dead," she tells Binx, "Now it's all up to you. It's going to be difficult for you but I know you're going to act like a soldier" (4).

21. Binx's participation in being is also underlined by his unwillingness to discuss it, for as Marcel asserts: "It is clear that the more I actually participate in being, the less I am capable of knowing or of saying in what it is that I participate" (*CF* 56).

22. A number of Binx's problems with fitting into the world stem from his relationship with his father, a troubled insomniac for whom nothing in life was worthwhile except war. Binx's unavailability, his refusal to open to others because he fears that too much may be required of him, results at least partly from his failed relationship with his father. Gabriel Marcel was very interested in the relationship between father and son because it provides a paradigm for God's love for his creatures. According to Marcel, the child is not an object belonging to the father in the realm of having, but a subject in the realm of being, a presence. The father's responsibility is to awaken his child to a consciousness of himself. In "The Creative Vow as the Essence of Fatherhood," Marcel warns that the father who sees his child as a person "to take his place or to make up to him one day for his personal inconveniences," reduces his child to object, cuts himself off from transcendence, and shuts his child out of the "closed system which he has formed with himself" (*HV* 120). Percy's interest in the search for the father appears in all his novels. Binx's "invincible unbelief," his inability to "make head or tail of God" would follow from his relationship with his father according to Marcel's system. If the human model of fatherhood fails to demonstrate love, how can anyone understand a loving God who is *like* a father?

Notes to Chapter Three

1. Will Barrett resembles his creator. In his introduction to *Lanterns on the Levee*, Percy describes himself as a youth "whose only talent was a knack for looking and listening, for tuning in and soaking up" (x).

2. In an interview with John Carr, Percy says that Will Barrett's father's suicide shocked Will so much that "he'd almost become a hysteric" (Lawson and Kramer, *Conversations* 67.)

3. Walker Percy, *The Last Gentleman* (New York: Farrar, Noonday, 1966) 18. Future references to this edition appear parenthetically in the text.

4. In an interview with Ashley Brown, Percy says, "[Barrett] is what Gabriel Marcel calls a *wayfarer*—like an old-fashioned pilgrim on a serious quest" (Lawson and Kramer, *Conversations* 13–14.) Percy tells Carlton Cremeens: "[Will Barrett] was on the move geographically and spiritually at the same time. It seemed appropriate for him to be moving. He is *homo viator* (Lawson and Kramer, *Conversations* 29).

5. In *Homo Viator*, Marcel discusses the importance of our placement in the social world in determining our understanding of ourselves. He states: "What concerns us here is only to know under what conditions I become conscious of myself as a person. It must be repeated that these conditions are essentially social" (*HV* 18).

6. In "The Loss of the Creature," Percy suggests various stratagems that may provide access to being; one of these is the "indirect approach," a sneaking up on being (*Message* 46–63). In "The Man on the Train," Percy discusses the accidental meeting which may make being accessible (*Message* 90).

7. Will Barrett fits Percy's description of the psychiatric patient for whom therapy will have little effect because of the likelihood that he will "fall prey to what Whitehead called the 'fallacy of misplaced concreteness' and so to bestow upon theory, or what he imagines to be theory, a superior reality at the expense of the reality of the very world he lives in. . . . His seduction by theory is such, however, as to place him almost beyond the reach of the therapist" (*Message* 211–12). Although Will Barrett believes in psychotherapy, he feels uncomfortable when he reads Dr. Gamow's clinical description of him as "a well-developed and nourished young white male . . . with a pleasing demeanor, dressed in an unusual raglan jacket" (39). Interestingly, Sutter's casebook opens with the shorthand for exactly this clinical phrase: "A w.d. and n. white male, circa 49" (279).

8. "A Talk with Walker Percy" in Lawson and Kramer, *Conversations* 82.

9. Percy tells Ashley Brown, "The reader is free to see [Will Barrett] as a sick man among healthy businessmen or as a sane pilgrim in a mad world" (Lawson and Kramer, *Conversations* 13).

10. An important event in Walker Percy's life is partially worked out in *The Last Gentleman*. When Walker was 13, his father LeRoy Pratt Percy committed suicide. Not surprisingly, the loss of the father is important in Percy's novels. Part of the characterization of Lawyer Ed Barrett is based on Walker Percy's "Uncle Will," William Alexander Percy. Lewis Baker's *The Percys of Mississippi: Politics and Literature in the New South* (Baton Rouge: Louisiana State University Press, 1983) provides an excellent background for understanding the Percy family, especially William Alexander Percy.

11. American Psychiatric Association, *Diagnostic and Statistical Manual of Mental Disorders*, 3rd ed. (Washington, D.C.: APA, 1980) 255–57.

12. "The Mystery of Language" in *Message* 156.

13. Percy explains to John Carr how he uses sex symbolically in his novels: "I take pleasure in turning Freud upside down. Instead of something being a symbol for sex in the Freudian style, I use sex as a symbol of something else. Sex [in *The Last Gentleman*] is a symbol of failure on the existential level" (Lawson and Kramer, *Conversations* 68).

14. Kitty Vaught fits Percy's description of the consumer self in "Notes for a Novel About the End of the World"—a self, "lost to himself in the rounds of consumership" (*Message* 115). Percy discusses the consumer self at length in "The Loss of the Creature" in *Message* 46–63.

15. See Percy's comments on the difference between the person who despairs and knows it and the one who does not even suspect that he despairs in "The Man on the Train" in *Message* 83–100.

16. Because Will is sleeping when Kitty kisses him, he incorporates Kitty into

his dream where she becomes an old girlfriend, Alice Bocock. Will must have known Alice when he was at Princeton since Flirtation Walk is at the United States Military Academy at West Point.

17. Percy is having fun here with Kitty's name. The alert reader will catch the reference to Katherine Gibbs, a secretarial school in Boston, known for turning out young women who, in addition to having good secretarial skills, know when to wear white gloves and how to conduct themselves like young ladies.

18. Ashley Brown, "An Interview with Walker Percy" in Lawson and Kramer, *Conversations* 14.

19. In his essay, "The Message in the Bottle," Percy suggests that "Come!" is a summons that will only be heeded by someone who is in a certain predicament: "If a man has lost his way in a cave and hears the cry 'Come! This way out!' the communication qualifies as news of high importance" (*Message* 131).

20. "Walker Percy's Indirect Communications," *Texas Studies in Literature and Language* 11 (1969): 899.

21. Will Barrett's experience with the hitching post reminds us of Binx's coming to himself in Korea and watching the dung beetle crawling around in front of him with the certainty that he was onto something, the possibility of a search. Percy agrees with Marcel that the Creator may be seen and loved in His creation. In *Being and Having*, Marcel notes the religious significance of the physical world: "My deepest and most unshakable conviction. . . . is that whatever all the thinkers and doctors have said, it is not God's will at all to be loved by us *against* the Creation, but rather glorified *through* the Creation and with the Creation as our starting point" (*BH* 135). Percy's novels are full of the wonder and joy to be found in the ordinary world. Reading Sutter's notebook, for example, makes Will feel disoriented. The ordinary experience of having his oil checked restores Will to the concrete world: "When the attendant brought over the dip stick, exhibiting its coating of good green Uniflow, slightly low, he savored the hot sane smell of the oil and felt in his own muscles the spring of the long sliver of steel" (282).

22. Both Marcel and Percy comment on the tendency of language that is often repeated to become devalued. Percy remarks that much of the vocabulary of religion is worn out: "the old words of grace are worn smooth as poker chips" (*Message* 116). Marcel observes, "Our world is more and more given over to the power of words, and of words that have been in a great measure emptied of their authentic content" (*MB* 1: 41).

Notes to Chapter Four

1. In "On the Ontological Mystery," an essay central to his thought, Marcel argues that the modern human being is "*at the mercy of his technics. . . . he is increasingly incapable of controlling his technics, or rather of controlling his own control.*" He goes on to assert that "*speaking metaphysically, the only genuine hope is hope in what does not depend on ourselves*, hope springing from humility and not from pride. . . . The proud man is cut off from a certain form of communion with his fellow man" (*PE* 31–32. Italics in original).

2. Walker Percy, *Love in the Ruins* (New York: Farrar, 1971) 18. Future references to this edition appear parenthetically in the text.

3. Percy says in an interview with John Griffin Jones that the novel is set in an area much like Covington, Louisiana, where he lives (Lawson and Kramer, *Conversations* 253).

4. Zoltan Abadi-Nagy puts the question to Percy, "Is not your third novel *Love in the Ruins* with its Layer I and Layer II—the social self and the inner individual self—a comic attempt to solve Marcel's dilemma about this separation?" Percy responds, "You are right. This is a comic device to get at what, ever since Kierkegaard, has been called the modern sickness: the disease of abstraction" (Lawson and Kramer, *Conversations* 73).

5. See, for example, Marcel's discussion in *Being and Having* where he says, "In turning my attention to what one usually thinks of as ontological problems, such as Does Being exist: What is Being? etc., I came to observe that I cannot think about these problems without seeing a new gulf open beneath my feet, namely, this I, I who ask questions about being, can I be sure that I exist: What qualifications do I have for pursuing these inquiries? (170).

6. In *The Philosophy of Existentialism*, Marcel clearly states the mysterious union of soul and body: "It is evident that there exists a mystery of the union of the body and the soul. The indivisible unity always inadequately expressed by such phrases as *I have a body, I make use of my body, I feel my body*, etc., can be neither analyzed nor reconstituted out of precedent elements" (19).

7. *Basic Writings: From "Being and Nothingness" (1927) to "The Task of Thinking" (1927)*, ed. and intro. David Farrell Krell (New York: Harper, 1977) 112.

8. See Lewis A. Lawson, "Tom More: Cartesian Physician," *Delta* (1981) 13: 67–83; and J. Gerald Kennedy, "The Sundered Self and the Riven World," in *The Art of Walker Percy: Stratagems for Being*, ed. Panthea Reid Broughton (Baton Rouge: Louisiana State University Press, 1979) 115–136.

9. Lawson, "Tom More: Cartesian Physician" 74.

10. Percy admits in an interview with Jan Nordby Gretland that Ellen didn't interest him very much: "My mother's family were Georgia Presbyterians. So I thought it would be nice to have a voluptuous Georgia Presbyterian girl. And she is not neurotic, she knows exactly what she wants. She may not be very deep; I wasn't too interested in her, I just wanted to have her there" (Lawson and Kramer, *Conversations* 212).

11. In the light of More's hope to save humankind with the lapsometer, one tenet of Calvinism seems especially appropriate—Calvin's argument that human beings can be saved only through the unmerited grace of God. We can do nothing to promote our salvation, and no amount of good works can further it.

12. William Roper, *The Life of Sir Thomas More* in *Two Early Tudor Lives*, eds. Richard S. Sylvester and Davis P. Harding (New Haven: Yale University Press, 1962) 239. Italics added.

13. E.E. Reynolds, *The Field Is Won: The Life and Death of St. Thomas More* (Milwaukee: Bruce, 1968) 221.

14. Giorgio de Santillana, ed., *The Age of Adventure* (New York: New American Library) 91.

Notes to Chapter Five

1. Lewis Lawson provides the chronology of John's visits in "Walker Percy's

Silent Character," *Mississippi Quarterly* 33 (Spring 1980): 123–140. In "The Fall of the House of Lamar," Lawson suggests that Harry's last name is probably Percy (Panthea Reid Broughton, ed. *The Art of Walker Percy: Stratagems for Being* (Baton Rouge: Louisiana State University Press, 1979) 43).

2. Walker Percy, *Lancelot* (New York: Farrar, 1977) 4–5. Future references to this edition appear parenthetically in the text.

3. "The Delta Factor" in *Message* 12.

4. *The Personalist* 41 (1960): 150.

5. Interview with John Griffin Jones in Lawson and Kramer, *Conversations* 281. In an interview with Jan Nordby Gretlund, Percy says that he originally wrote a dialogue between Lancelot and John, but that the priest did not work, so he wrote him out (Lawson and Kramer, *Conversations* 210).

6. Walker Percy, "Notes for a Novel About the End of the World" in *Message* 116.

7. The mirror metaphor is tied closely in this novel to the metaphor of the photographic negative. When Lancelot views videotapes his servant Elgin has prepared for him, he discovers that they are distorted with "lights and darks . . . reversed like a negative" (185).

8. Simon Vauthier calls attention to the doubling in the novel in "Story, Story-Teller and Listener: Notes on *Lancelot*," *South Carolina Review* 13 (1981): 39–54.

9. Percy's epigraph appears on the unnumbered page preceding the title page. John Cunningham points out that while the epigraph can refer only ambiguously to Lancelot, it aptly describes the priest ["The Thread in the Labyrinth: *Love in the Ruins* and One Tradition of Comedy," *South Carolina Review* 13 (1981): 33].

10. *Message* 83.

11. "Story, Story-Teller and Listener: Notes on *Lancelot*" 41–42.

12. See Percy's discussion in "Toward a Triadic Theory of Meaning" in *Message* 159–188.

13. "Walker Percy's Silent Character" 129.

14. In an interview with Jan Nordby Gretlund, Percy says, "[*Lancelot*] is supposed to be a very conventional, classical statement of two different traditions. . . . Aunt Emily on the one side [representing the Greco-Roman tradition] and orthodox Christianity on the other" (Lawson and Kramer, *Conversations* 211).

15. With his emphasis on orgasm as the only vehicle for transcending self, Lancelot resembles Sutter Vaught.

16. Cleanth Brooks, "Walker Percy and Modern Gnosticism" in *The Art of Walker Percy*, ed. Panthea Reid Broughton, 260–272. Lewis A. Lawson, "The Gnostic Vision in *Lancelot*," *Renascence* 32 (1979): 52–64.

17. Walker Percy is familiar with Marcel's thoughts about mass movements. In an interview with Jan Nordby Gretlund, Percy describes the experiences that led to his portrayal of Lance's "new order": "I spent a summer in Germany in 1934, and I lived with a family in Bonn. The father was a member of the S.A., *Schutz Abwehr*, and the son was a member of *Hitlerjugend*. There was a tremendous excitement at the 'rejuvenation' of Germany. . . . Perhaps I was also thinking of Gabriel Marcel, he is French, a Jew, a Catholic convert, who had the nerve to say: we tend to overlook something positive about the mass movements. It is easy to say how wrong they were. It is easy to overlook the positive things: the great sense of verve

and vitality. This I was very much aware of in Germany in 1934. It made it even more seductive" (Lawson and Kramer, *Conversations* 208). Percy tells John Griffin Jones: "Marcel always talked about being wary of mass movements or causes. There's always a danger of taking up a cause, of being too much identified with a cause" (Lawson and Kramer, *Conversations* 277–78).

Notes to Chapter Six

1. Percy tells John Griffin Jones that he had written the first third of *The Second Coming* before he realized who the protagonist was: "After [a] hundred pages or so I realized it was Will Barrett; at least with a couple of changes I was able to make it Will Barrett very easily. It couldn't have been anybody else, so I became aware it was Will Barrett" (Lawson and Kramer, *Conversations* 281).

2. Walker Percy, *The Second Coming* (New York: Farrar, 1980) 290. Future references to this edition appear parenthetically in the text.

3. Walker Percy made up both name and treatment for Will Barrett's condition. See Ben Forkner and J. Gerald Kennedy, "An Interview with Walker Percy" in Lawson and Kramer, *Conversations* 236.

4. See Marcel's discussion of "my death" in *Creative Fidelity* 140–150.

5. "The Semiotics of Memory: Suicide in *The Second Coming*," *Delta* 13 (1981): 106.

6. "The Semiotics of Memory" 118. In an interview with James Atlas, Percy comments on Will Barrett's position: "[Will is] facing death. It's only the prospect of death that enables him to act at last" (Lawson and Kramer, *Conversations* 183).

7. The "hunting accident" left Will Barrett with a permanently damaged middle ear and a scar on his cheek which is remarkably like Sutter Vaught's scar. When Allie sees Will approaching her greenhouse, she notices that "a shadow like a German saber scar crossed one cheek" (*SC* 106). Sutter's scar is described in almost identical language: "There was something wrong with his cheek, a distinguished complication like a German saber scar" (*LG* 207).

8. "The Semiotics of Memory" 107.

9. For Percy's discussion of the man who worries that the bomb will not fall, see "The Man on the Train" in *Message* 84–85.

10. See William Rodney Allen, *Walker Percy: A Southern Wayfarer* (Jackson: University Press of Mississippi, 1986). Allen argues that Will Barrett's fascination with the last days comes "from within himself." Allen thoughtfully explores the importance of Will's father's suicide.

11. *Walker Percy: A Southern Wayfarer* 132–33.

12. It is extremely interesting that Percy chose to afflict Will Barrett with a toothache. In his essay "The Ego and Its Relation to Others," Marcel discusses the ego: "Burdened with myself, plunged in this disturbing world . . . I keep an eager look-out for everything emanating from it which might either soothe or ulcerate the wound I bear within me, which is my *ego*. This state is strikingly analogous to that of a man who has an abscess at the root of his tooth and who experiments cautiously with heat and cold, acid and sugar to get relief" (*HV* 16). Percy's familiarity with this essay is apparent from his frequent references to ideas it contains. For example, in "Symbol as Hermeneutic in Existentialism," Percy refers to Marcel's "aching wound of self" (*Message* 283–84).

13. The importance of incarnation in Marcel's philosophy has already been noted. According to Marcel, a person who can say neither "I *am* a body" nor "I *have* a body" exists midway between being and having, participating in both realms. Walker Percy is also concerned with this modern inability to acknowledge our own presences as bodies. In *Lost in the Cosmos*, Percy discusses "the loneliness of self, stranded as it is in an unspeakable consciousness in a world from which it perceives itself as somehow estranged, stranded even within its own body, with which it sees no clear connection" (180).

14. Percy says in an interview with Edmund Fuller that he is pleased with his creation of Allie Huger (Lawson and Kramer, *Conversations* 188). Allie is the only female character Percy has developed from within, allowing her to be a point-of-view character for part of the novel. Percy has remarked that of all his characters, Kate Cutrer is in some ways most like him. See John Griffin Jones's interview in Lawson and Kramer, *Conversations* 282. It is likely that Allie also shares some of her creator's temperament.

15. Jo Gulledge, "The Reentry Option: An Interview with Walker Percy" in Lawson and Kramer, *Conversations* 307.

16. Allie's notebook may be contrasted with the notebook Sutter Vaught keeps in *The Last Gentleman*. Sutter's notebook is full of disillusionment with himself and the times. It is of no real use to him in living a life. Allie's notebook, on the other hand, has a life-affirming purpose. When Allie writes things down, she has a way to live until her memory recovers from the shock treatment.

17. See Robert Coles, *Walker Percy: An American Search* (Boston: Little, 1978). Coles comments on the I/thou in every individual: "Percy's repetition, akin to Marcel's 'recollection' and a modification of Kierkegaard's version of repetition, has the contemporary 'I' meeting up with a former version of itself: one's former self thereby becomes a 'thou'" (98).

18. Percy uses Marcel's designations, problem and mystery, a number of times in the novel. For example, Allie herself is introduced as "a little problem" that confronts her mother Kitty Vaught (66). Allie has legal title to the island Kitty wants to sell to an Arab. Kitty's "little problem" would be resolved if Allie were to be found incompetent. Young Will Barrett also found himself confronted with a problem when his father attempted suicide. Although what happened to Will on the Georgia hunting trip was really a mystery in which he was himself involved, 12-year-old Will suffered traumatic shock when his father wounded him and then turned the gun on himself. Protected by shock which caused him to disassociate from the mystery of what had happened, Will saw his critically wounded father as a problem: "Now [Will] was blowing into his hands and thinking: This is a problem and problems are for solving" (58).

19. *The Personalist* 41 (1960): 155. Percy also discusses the unformulable self in "Symbol as Hermeneutic in Existentialism" in *Message* 277–287. The entire "intermesso" section of *Lost in the Cosmos* (83–126) deals with the unspeakableness of the self to itself from a semiotic point of view. Gabriel Marcel makes a similar point about the basic unformulability of the self when he notices that so often the responses an individual provides on a form do not indicate who he is: "I have not a consciousness of *being* the person who is entered under the various headings thus: *son of, born at, occupation,* and so on. Yet everything I enter under these headings is strictly true" (*MB* 1: 103–4).

20. "Naming and Being," *The Personalist* 41 (1960): 155.

21. All the allusions have something to do with death. Leo Tolstoy requested that he be buried near the spot where his older brother, Nikolai, told him he had hidden a green stick on which were written the words that would make all men brothers [Ernest J. Simmons, *Leo Tolstoy* (Boston: Little, 1946) 21–22]. "Green stick" is a particularly aptly chosen allusion, echoing as it does the choice Will Barrett has to make between *thanatos* represented by his father's Greener and *eros* represented by Allie's greenhouse. Edgar Allen Poe's short story "The Gold Bug" revolves around a death's-head, buried treasure, and two skeletons that are discovered with the treasure chest. "Rosebud" is the dying word spoken by the protagonist in the film *Citizen Kane*. Ernest Hemingway saw in the matador an embodiment of courage in the deliberate risking of death.

22. Leon Edel, *Henry James, The Master: 1901–1916* (New York: Lippincott, 1972) 542. These words are often reported as James's last. It makes a good story, but his actual words were far more prosaic and human. According to Edel, James's last intelligible words, uttered on February 25, were addressed to his sister-in-law: "Stay with me, Alice, stay with me" (560). Henry James died on 28 February 1916.

23. Walker Percy, "Questions They Never Asked Me *So He Asked Them Himself*" in Lawson and Kramer, *Conversations* 175.

24. Ben Forkner and J. Gerald Kennedy, "An Interview with Walker Percy" in Lawson and Kramer, *Conversations* 234.

25. *Walker Percy: A Southern Wayfarer* 151.

Notes to Chapter Seven

1. William Rodney Allen, *Walker Percy: A Southern Wayfarer* xii. Allen focuses on Percy's novels as they embody Percy's "response to the trauma of his father's suicide." Allen bases his discussion of the novels on the broader context of the pattern of decline from grandfather to father to son in southern families which Richard King establishes in *A Southern Renaissance* (New York: Oxford University Press, 1980).

2. *Walker Percy* (Boston: G.K. Hall, 1983) iii.

3. Walker Percy, *The Thanatos Syndrome* (New York: Farrar, 1987) 365. Future references to this edition appear parenthetically in the text.

4. Internal references suggest a time in the mid-nineties. Lucy Lipscomb says that her Uncle Hugh Bob hasn't done anything in the "fifty years" since World War II (143). More mentions the arrival of Americans "two hundred years ago in 1796" (161), and he remembers watching *As the World Turns* "over thirty years ago" when it was interrupted by a bulletin announcing that President Kennedy had been shot (203). Near the end of the novel Father Smith says, "In a few years this dread century will be over" (365). Although the numbers are no doubt approximations, there are enough references to suggest that the year is around 1995, perhaps 1996.

5. John Edward Hardy points out that the dates don't fit and that More would have had to be only ten years old when studying under Sullivan [*The Fiction of Walker Percy* (Urbana: University of Illinois Press, 1987) 227–28].

6. Hardy 244.

7. See the interview by Phil McCombs, "Century of Thanatos: Walker Percy

and His 'Subversive Message'," *The Southern Review* 11 (Autumn 1988): 809–10, for Percy's remarks on his visit to Germany with his German professor from the University of North Carolina.

8. Clearly Percy has invented a Supreme Court Decision to echo *Roe v. Wade* (1973) which permits abortion in the first trimester of pregnancy. The determination that "personhood" begins around the age of 18 months shows that Percy is up on current medical thinking. In *The Mind*, Richard M. Restak writes, "The third major milestone—one that distinguishes us from all other species—is the growth of a sense of self, self-consciousness, self-awareness," adding that between 18 and 24 months, children "become aware that they have intentions, that they have feelings, that they can act" (61). This sense of self develops at the same time that children are rapidly learning language.

9. *The Mind* (New York: Bantam, 1988) 83. Italics added.

10. Gabriel Marcel, *Tragic Wisdom and Beyond*, trans. Stephen Jolin and Peter McCormick (Evanston: Northwestern University Press, 1973) 108. Future references to this edition, abbreviated as *TW*, appear parenthetically in the text.

11. Current research indicates that although chimpanzees can be taught words and can even produce sentences along the order of "Sarah cut apple," they manipulate words as things (literally plastic chips in one experiment) and never develop either grammatical or syntactical ability. Chimps lack the ability to abstract. After three and a half decades of working with chimpanzees, Dr. David Premack concludes "there's not the slightest indication the pieces of plastic taught the animal have in any way entered its head, and become part of the system which is used for the representation of language. That contrasts powerfully with the human case, where we have very good reason to suppose that quite interesting things are going on inside the head with the use of language" (*The Mind* 203).

12. "East Coker," ll. 89–90.

13. Flannery O'Connor, *Mystery and Manners* (New York: Farrar, 1962) 227. Gabriel Marcel employs the same metaphor. Warning that when the individual is seen mechanistically, as a collection of "functions," he will have no other reality, Marcel writes: "There lies a road which runs straight to the forced labor camp and the cremation oven" (*MB* 2: 165).

14. Marcel vehemently opposed the idea that the human being could ever become God's collaborator because he understood that "The rather vague idea of man's completion of the work begun by God seems part of our mental atmosphere today" (*TW* 115).

15. In *The Philosophy of Existentialism*, Marcel calls attention to the dangers of the abstraction, *Das Volk*: "It must not be forgotten that the Fascist dictatorships, whether in Germany, Italy or elsewhere, similarly exalted 'the people' and offered it a ceaseless and cheap adulation; yet what contempt did not this adulation conceal, and to what abject depth did they not reduce their citizens" (85–86).

16. McCombs 816.

17. Hardy 245.

18. Father Smith officiates at the reopening of St. Margaret's hospice on January 5, the feast day of St. Simeon Stylites. He runs the hospice for a while and then retires once again to the tower. It must be January 5 of the next year when Ellen takes Father Smith's message, asking More to assist him the next day, January 6, in celebrating Mass.

19. Jac Tharpe, *Walker Percy* 119.

20. John Edward Hardy has noticed Percy's emphasis on the apocalypse and observes of Tom More's apocalyptic yearnings at the end of *Love in the Ruins*: "The trouble with Tom More's, as with most if not all millenarian thinking, is in his evident impatience to see the end" (*The Fiction of Walker Percy* 125).

21. Hardy 136.

22. In *Metaphysical Journal* Marcel remarks, "The bizarre expression that comes to my mind for stating this is that, while an empirical 'thou' can be converted to a 'him', God is the absolute 'thou' who can never become a 'him'" (137).

23. Lawson and Kramer, *Conversations* 176.

24. McCombs 812.

Notes to Afterword

1. Walker Percy, "The State of the Novel: Dying Art or New Science?" *Michigan Quarterly Review* 16 (Fall 1977): 371.

2. "The State of the Novel" 372.

3. "Naming and Being," *The Personalist* 41 (1960): 156.